D0752850

I
WASN'T
READY

by

John S. Munday

with

Frances Wohlenhaus-Munday

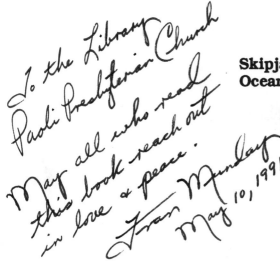

To the Library
Paoli Presbyterian Church
May all who read
this book reach out
in love & peace.
Fran Munday
May 10, 1991

Skipjack Press, Inc.
Ocean City, Maryland

Scripture quotations are from the REVISED STANDARD VERSION BIBLE, COPYRIGHT 1946, 1952, 1971 by the Division of Christian Education of the National Council of the Churches of Christ in the USA and used with permission.
The poem, "Stepping Stones," on pages 42 & 43 is reprinted with permission of the author, Barbara Williams.

COVER ART: KATHY MUMFORD, Ocean City, MD

Library of Congress Cataloging in Publication Data:

Munday, John S., 1940-
    I Wasn't Ready
      1. Healing grief   2. Theology
      3. Counselling   4. Death of a child

ISBN 1-879-535-01-7   Paper

Published by SKIPJACK PRESS, INC.
               OCEAN CITY, MARYLAND

Printed in the United States of America

3234

MARLYS ANN WOHLENHAUS
JANUARY 11, 1961 - MAY 10, 1979

Dedicated to Marlys

Turn around, turn around,
think of all the good times that
we've had.
Turn around just once more,
think of all the good times, not the bad.
There's always time for living
But I guess this means goodbye.
I know it's very hard to do
But I guess I'll have to try.
I've seen you for the last time,
But I won't see you again.
I loved you as my sister
And I loved you as my friend.
I hope they find the person
That committed such a crime.
He took your life away from you,
He'll serve a lot of time.
Life is too important
To be taken in a day.
We tried to bring you back to us
In each and every way.
I know that you're in heaven
And there's something you should know
That even though you had to die
I didn't want to let you go.

Lynn
May 11, 1979

iii

ACKNOWLEDGMENTS

We would like to thank the following people who have been so important in our lives and who gave of themselves to make this book possible.

Raymond W. Wohlenhaus and Lynn Wohlenhaus Winger, Fran's surviving children, have suffered the loss of their sister Marlys. Their grief did not stop them from reaching out to Mom in love.

John D. Munday, Maria Munday Stine and Shawn A. Munday, Jack's children, never had the chance to call Marlys "sister." Their patience and love from the outside is treasured.

The Reverend Richard Borgstrom, retired pastor of the Memorial Lutheran Church in Afton, Minnesota, gave us words of wisdom and comfort that took on greater meaning as the years went by.

Our many friends at the Valley Forge, Pa. Chapter of The Compassionate Friends, Inc. gave us accompaniment on the journey to healing.

Professor J. Deotis Roberts, of Eastern Baptist Theological Seminary, gave wisdom and insight to us both in several classes and as a friend. Professor J. Christaan Beker, of Princeton Theological Seminary, gave us further insight in his class and his book, *Suffering and Hope.*

Rolland W. Tapp, Ph.D., gave us his guidance and editorial skill during the writing of this book.

Artist Kathy Lynn Mumford captured beautifully the concept of the butterfly, the symbol of new life. Kathy teaches art to children and adults. She lives with her husband and son in Ocean City, Maryland.

INTRODUCTION

Books written by parents whose child has died are often beautifully told from the perspective of the child and the events surrounding his or her death. For every child who dies before the parents, there is a story of an unfinished life. This book is more. *I Wasn't Ready* is the story of healing, told in loving memory of one child, Marlys Ann Wohlenhaus.

This book is a story of hope, found in the understanding that if we can't have our child back, we can be healed. While we never are the same person after the child dies, and in that sense we never recover, we can be healed. Our child would want us to be healed.

It is the story of her mother's struggle to survive the grief which she and every bereaved parent endures. It is a story of her faith in God and her faith in God's comfort during this most difficult time in life.

And, this book is a story of love. Love exists in the midst of grief, and finding that love is the key to healing. Healing does take place only when we reach out in love. Love

v

for others, placing others ahead of ourselves, brings healing.

I Wasn't Ready is a book about hope, and faith and love. Hope for healing. Faith in God. Love for others, that they too may be healed. Marlys would have wanted that for her mother. Her mother, and all parents who are bereaved, want that for all the world.

Fran is a bereaved parent, and will always be one. But the recovery process is real, and offers much. We hope that this book will answer questions that every bereaved parent has asked themselves and others.

Jack is not a bereaved parent, and he has struggled to understand something that goes beyond any intellectual knowledge. This book is intended to bring comfort and understanding for those who don't know the pain of bereavement.

This book is our way of healing as we reach out to our readers in love.

Fran and Jack Munday
Ocean City, Maryland

CONTENTS

1

YOU NEVER EXPECT IT TO HAPPEN

It happens. Out of the blue, out of nowhere, someone you love dies. Someone close dies. A child dies. Your child.

Even when you hear of someone's child dying, you close your mind to the horror because you never expect it to happen. But, then, it does! There must be a mistake, you think. Not your child. Not dead. No. No.

Marlys Ann Wohlenhaus was brutally attacked with a blunt instrument, suffering blows to her head. The time was approximately 2:40 p.m., on Tuesday, May 8, 1979. Marlys was in the safety of her home. Her mother found her less than an hour later, lying in a pool of blood. No one ever expected it to happen.

* * *

At the time of her murder, Marlys was 18 years old and a senior at Stillwater High

School, in Stillwater, Minnesota. On Saturday, May 12th, Marlys was buried at the little white church on the hill in Afton. The next day was Mother's Day. Fran cried all day.

The church cemetery looks down on the St. Croix River as it forms the border between Minnesota and neighboring Wisconsin. Marlys had been confirmed at Memorial Lutheran Church where she attended regularly.

This book tells the story of Marlys Ann Wohlenhaus's murder. This book is also the story of her mother's grief and the healing path that her mother has traveled. It is the story of how Marlys's mother, Fran, lived through that most unthinkable experience of finding her daughter, dying, in her own home. It is a story of Christian response to murder. And that very difficult path that leads to healing.

Some days after the murder, after the rest of the world had gone back to being normal, in a moment of anguish and vocal expression of her grief over Marlys's murder, Fran cried out, "I wasn't ready to let her go."

* * *

No one really ever is ready to let go, especially of his or her child. But the sudden shock of the death of a child, in a complete and permanent way, subjects the parents to grief which is unlike any other experience in life.

There are far too many parents who know that grief. Those who truly know the pain that brings forth the cry, "I wasn't ready to let her go," reach out to fellow travelers, to offer something to hold on to. This book is the story of those who experience the unexpected. This is the story of a mother who has lived with what experts say is the most difficult pain to experience.

It is also the story of efforts to understand that grief by one, not her parent, whose life has also been forever changed by Marlys's murder. It is a book for the bereaved parent and it is also a book for those who would comfort those who mourn.

Throughout the past eleven years, Fran has said many times that her faith has kept her sane through all the grief. This is a theology of accompaniment, which this book will share with you, which explains how faith works in the lives of bereaved parents, parents who grieve in the death of their child, to bring hope of healing. Healing does come, in accompaniment by and with others who also suffer. Theology is often given a name, and we have chosen "accompaniment" as the name for the theology of this book. As the bereaved parent knows only too well, being there is the only hope for recovery.

As with most explanations of God's action in the lives of humans, this theology begins with the story of what happened. It is essential for the parent to be able to tell the world and those who would listen that their child has died. Their child is dead.

The parent who has suffered the death of a child needs to tell the story of the child and the death. Everything begins with the story. What happened? And how did it happen? Why did it happen?

Marlys died from a violent and vicious attack, and those details have to be part of the story. If she had been killed in an auto accident or had been the victim of cancer, that would have been part of this book. For the parent whose child dies, everything is part of the story that must be told.

In the story, in the telling and re-telling sometimes, one finds that God has been present too. But first, it is necessary to tell the story.

*   *   *

On that horrible day, Fran found her daughter Marlys in the small office in their home shortly after 3:30 p.m., as Fran returned from a shopping trip. Fran remembers looking at her watch, noting the time. Her younger daughter, Lynn, was not due home from school for another ten

4

minutes, too long to wait at the end of the long driveway. Fran drove up to the house and saw Marlys's car as she expected. Nothing seemed unusual.

Fran remembers every detail of the events that followed. As she went into the house, through the unlocked ground level door, she called to her daughter. She remembers noticing that the family Saint Bernard did not come bounding up to greet her, and thought that Marlys must have just let her out. Later, the dog, Patience, was found upstairs, closed in Fran's bedroom, where she would have gone to avoid anyone who came into the house except close family. The killer apparently was able to shut the door and confine the dog.

Fran thought that Marlys was on the phone when Marlys didn't answer her call. Fran remembers carrying a package, her purse, and some mail she had picked up in town. She remembers putting the package and her purse down on the stairs to the upper level and walking toward the small office. She remembers noticing that the door to a spare room was open. The door had been closed when Fran left home that morning. The killer apparently was able to hide in that room until Marlys went into the little office.

Fran will never forget the scene in the office where she found Marlys, dying, in a

5

pool of her own blood. She will never forget finding Marlys facing the huge roll-top desk, her purse at her feet, lying by the desk with the mail where Marlys put it in what was probably her last conscious act.

Fran immediately called the ambulance through the Washington County Sheriff's dispatcher. She remembers how she was calm and clear in her description and directions, and how she was not calm in expressing her urgency. She remembers yelling to the Sheriff to use the side door because the front door was locked.

Fran tried to give Marlys aid as she waited the few minutes it took the ambulance crew to arrive. They were soon on the scene and took Marlys to one of the finest emergency hospitals anywhere. Every effort was made to save her at the Saint Paul Ramsey Medical Center Hospital.

Fran also called a friend, John Munday, who has since become her husband. At about 3:45 p.m., he received a phone call in his office in Minneapolis from Fran. That call, and the haunting voice he heard, is still running around in his head, probably never to be forgotten. "Jack! Oh, Jack! If I ever needed you, I need you now. It's Marlys. It's bad. Come now. Don't wait."

After briefly talking, just long enough to know where to go, Jack drove as fast as he could to Fran's home. He saw the ambulance on its way to the hospital as he raced toward Afton. Jack met Fran a short distance from her house, as she was in another car being taken to the emergency room. She transferred to his car and Fran described the horror of finding her daughter, Marlys.

Marlys never had a chance. Fran said that in the car. The doctors said that as well. Two days later, on Thursday, May 10, 1979, Marlys was declared officially dead and her wish to be a donor was honored.

The murder is still unsolved.

2

I WANT TO BE HEALED

It was a long time before Fran could shut her eyes and not see Marlys lying in her blood in that office. She will never forget that sight.

The murder has never been solved. Fran has come to accept that it may never be solved and that the killer may not be punished by a court of law. Fran has come to accept a lot of things. She has almost come to accept that Marlys is dead. She has learned to live with her grief, as the pain comes much less often, and, perhaps, less intense. She will never stop missing Marlys.

Fran says that her faith in God has kept her sane. It has not been easy. In truth, it was not until she found others who had experienced the tragedy of the death of a child that she started to heal. Real healing began when she started to help others.

Fran is not an expert. She has not formally been trained in grief counseling.

Fran says, "I do not have all the answers, but I do know one thing. Grief is never over. It only erupts less frequently as time goes on."

Grief is a pain that one cannot physically touch. It is a pain where there is emptiness, as when an arm has been amputated. One knows that the arm has been cut off, and one doesn't consciously think about it being gone every minute of the day. But it is still gone. One can control the loss and can live a fairly complete life without the arm, but one can't ever expect life to be the way it was before.

*　*　*

It is a fair question to ask how Fran's faith has helped her stay sane. Both Fran and Jack have searched the Hebrew Scriptures, the New Testament, and writings by religious people of many faiths. They admit that there is no magic verse or sayings that takes away the pain of one's loss. There is no religious doctrine that has helped Fran to fully understand her feelings. Many times she has asked, "Where is God in all this?"

For some, religion is not an answer to their pain. A father whose son died in a car accident says, "There is no God. Besides, I hate God." They have no answer to his anguish but they have taken the time to sit with him, and let him rage. They have even added some of their own complaints to God.

But Fran does get comfort from her faith. She realizes that she cannot survive this terrible loss alone. She needs help, and to be honest, always will need help.

One source of help is the comfort that can be found from special verses in Scripture. These verses are special because they give comfort or joy or contentment. The truth contained in the verses resonates with the understanding that is drawn from life experiences.

One such verse in the Bible was learned from a friend, a pastor, a man who deals with the grief and pain of the homeless and the victims of war in Nicaragua. He has seen pain, too. He says that when grief and pain are too much for the moment, he goes for a walk.

Their friend recites this verse from Isaiah 61: 3 when he walks:

> *He gave me beauty for ashes,*
> *the oil of joy for mourning,*
> *a garment of praise*
> *for the spirit of heaviness.*
> *I am a tree of righteousness,*
> *a planting of the Lord,*
> *that He might be glorified.*

Neither Fran nor Jack can say that verse, or sing it as their friend taught them, without feeling a little bit better.

The Bible verses may not give them answers to the questions that they want to ask. It may not tell them why Marlys was murdered. It won't explain the actions of the killer in terms that can be understood. It won't explain why some children get cancer and others don't. Those questions have no real answers.

A theology professor told Jack there are no answers. The professor's son was killed by a drunken driver, and he said, "There are no answers, but you know that. You are a fellow traveler." Fellow travelers reach out to each other, accompany each other when the need is greatest. They do not let the lack of concrete and understandable answers prevent the healing process from beginning.

* * *

The theology of accompaniment acknowledges that fellow travelers want to help each other begin to heal and reduce the pain of their grief. By reaching out, by simply being there for others, there is healing. Grief-stricken and tormented souls slowly become aware that others are there with them. In time, even without answers, they begin to want to be healed, taking that first step that leads to other steps and healing.

There is a biblical story that is helpful to understand the importance of wanting to be healed. It is from John 5: 2-9, as follows:

"Now there is in Jerusalem by the Sheep Gate a pool, in Hebrew called Beth-zatha, which has five porticoes. In these lay a multitude of invalids, blind, lame, paralyzed. One man was there, who had been ill for thirty-eight years. When Jesus saw him and knew that he had been lying there a long time, he said to him, "Do you want to be healed?" The sick man answered him, "Sir, I have no man to put me into the pool when the water is troubled, and while I am going another steps down before me." Jesus said to him, "Rise, take up your pallet, and walk." And at once the man was healed, and he took up his pallet and walked."

The comfort in this Scripture is not that there will be a miracle. The expectation of the sick man is not that his paralysis will be cured. Certainly, for those who read these verses, there is no promise that their child who has died will be given back to them. The hope of these verses is that healing is something that has to be wanted. The question that is asked is, "Do you want to be healed?"

Fran's father died suddenly when she was nine years old. She prayed then for God to bring him back to life. Fran says, "I begged, pleaded, bargained, and cried, and my father did not come back." When Marlys was murdered, she prayed again for God to answer her prayer and give her back. She begged, pleaded, bargained, and cried. Marlys did not come back.

In time, Fran realized that praying for miracles like bringing Marlys back was not going to help her deal with her grief. Sure, she wanted her back, and always will. But now she knows that in this world that doesn't happen. Fran also wants to be healed. She doesn't want to be paralyzed by her grief, wanting only the return of her daughter. Fran now says, "If Marlys can't come back to me, I want to be healed."

3

AT FIRST, IT IS UNBEARABLE

There is no doubt that intense grief brings intense pain to those who mourn. The death of a child brings grief that comes like waves of a storm that cannot be controlled. At first, the pain is unbearable, and then it gets worse.

Initially, the pain which is felt when a child dies is protected by shock. As shock wears off, the pain can be hidden in denial, or the pain can be absorbed in anger. In time, when the child's death is accepted as fact, when it is faced with acceptance, or at least resignation, the pain feels worse. After shock, anger and denial have ceased to act as protection from reality, the pain is still there.

After Marlys was attacked, the ambulance crew rushed her to the emergency room. There was so much confusion. Fran was disoriented and in shock. As the reality began to penetrate into her mind, she began to experience unbearable pain. That was the beginning of a long, long time when she was in pain. Fran realizes now that during the first couple of years after Marlys was murdered, she endured many forms of that pain.

Whenever Fran closed her eyes, she would see Marlys as she first found her, on the floor in a pool of blood. It was a vision that she thought would never be erased from her mind's eye. Going to bed became torture because it meant closing her eyes. Stopping to think about a task she was doing to occupy her mind brought the paralyzing sight back. How could she pray when just closing her eyes brought back the pain her prayers were intended to heal?

Even when the vision became less frequent, the certainty that it would come back brought another kind of pain. Even now, more than eleven years after Marlys's murder, the vision comes once in a while. Those are the bad days, but they are not every day any more.

What is important to know for the bereaved is that healing does take place. There will be times when sleep will come without pain and concentration will return so that necessary work and even fun things can be done. There will be a time again when prayer is a comfort and a reminder that God has been present and active in the healing process.

What is important for others, for those who would offer beauty for ashes and the oil of joy for mourning, is that time for healing belongs to the bereaved. It is the parent of the child who has the pain. The rest of the world cannot see the visions of horror. Others don't have the ability to let in the pain. The task of the others is to be understanding without having a real understanding. It is not easy to comfort those who mourn. It is not easy to understand pain which is not experienced. The time for healing really does belong to the grieving parent who is feeling the pain. Time belongs to the bereaved because they cannot describe what is unbearable. They cannot describe the pain.

*   *   *

The hospital emergency scene was chaotic. Marlys was already in surgery and Fran was just starting to realize the full horror of what she had encountered. Jack had not seen Marlys or the pool of blood. He was trying to stop rejecting the words he heard. A barrier had already been formed between Fran and Jack. Marlys's death was a reality. Fran's pain was just beginning for her. There was no way for Jack to understand.

The hospital was so real. The doctors were totally absorbed with saving Marlys. The police, who wanted statements from everybody, were not less serious than the doctors. Murder is as real as anything in life, and yet it was so hard to understand.

Many times since that emergency room scene, Fran and Jack have talked about how hard it is to accept a tragedy like this. Fran's call for help is still vivid in Jack's memory, but at that time he couldn't comprehend the words. They both clearly remember the ride to the hospital, or rather remember talking, trying to understand the meaning of Fran's words, "There is no hope."

"You don't know that. The doctors will do all they can," Jack replied.

"You didn't see her. I did! I will probably always see her like that. There was bone, and blood, and parts of her."

Fran wasn't crying now. That would come later, but now she was still trying to comprehend what her eyes saw. Fran was having her first experience with the difficulty she would have in expressing what she saw.

Jack was offering comfort, but from a perspective that could not see. Jack did not see what Fran saw, and could not see it as she did, even if he had been in the little office with Fran when Marlys was found. And being blind to the vision, he began his first experience with the difficulty he would have in understanding the words he heard.

Eventually, the barrier that was formed that day has been lowered, almost completely. Understanding is almost possible for those who have not felt the pain of a bereaved parent, and those parents almost believe that the others do understand.

Eventually, it did get there, Jack says, but not without sacrificial caring. "The hardest thing I have ever done was to bring the realization that Marlys is dead into my heart and my mind and my understanding, never in this life to ever be here with me." Fran almost believes him.

*   *   *

What Fran remembers most about the hospital is the kindness that the nurses and doctors had for her. She remembers that it seemed like there were a dozen of them, doing what they could to comfort her as she watched the monitors, looking for a sign of hope. Teams of specialists worked hard and Fran remembers how caring they were as they explained each step, each option, each significant event. Fran remembers the hospital staff being a comfort, and even more than a comfort. The hospital staff was a physical support for her, keeping her in some condition to deal with the steps being taken

1 8

and the medical results, or lack of medical progress.

During the second day at the hospital, it became clear that there was no hope. Marlys would never recover. She was brain dead. Nothing could be done to restore her life. Even then, the doctors and staff were a comfort as they worked to prepare Marlys for becoming a donor.

The fact that Marlys would be a donor, was a great comfort to Fran. She and Marlys had talked about that possibility and Marlys had placed the donor authorization on her driver's license when she reached the age of 18. This act would give life and hope to others.

Fran still remembers that time in the hospital. She says, "I remember being like a zombie, being unable to function, and being comforted. The pain was unbearable at first. I remember the comfort and hard work of the hospital staff as they prepared Marlys to be a donor, after there was no hope at all. Psalm 23 says, *Thy rod and thy staff, they comfort me.'* I know, 'The hospital staff, they comforted me.' Looking back, I find God in that comfort."

4

WE DESPAIRED OF LIFE ITSELF

The experiences of grief are very jagged and erratic during the first years after the loss of a child. There are so many feelings that come during this time. Low self esteem, preoccupation, guilt, anger, loneliness, sadness, helplessness, despair, physical symptoms, sobbing and crying, shock, denial, repetition, telling the story over and over, confusion, idealization, anxiety and panic, bargaining and severe depression.

Also, there is envy, frustration, resentment, bitterness, and hatred. Most of all is the constant pain that comes from simply missing the child. All of those things happen, sometimes over and over, again and again.

Sobbing is an outlet for the deep strong emotions that accompany the death of a loved one. It is easier for women, but men sob, deeply sob, perhaps only in the dark of night, in their bed, alone. Some people cry often and cry a lot, while others push down their tears. Fran says, "I think it is helpful to cry, to sob, to release all the emotion that builds up. I didn't do enough of that, because I didn't think others would understand."

No one can really feel those emotions for another. Many times, when both parents of a child who has died try to talk with each other about what they feel, they find that they are at different places in their grieving. The inability to express what is seen and felt is common to everyone. Each spouse is totally consumed with what he or she feel individually, that there is no room for extending comfort to the other. That will come later as they discover the similarities of their healing process.

* * *

At the moment of the death of a child, whether by murder as Marlys died, or by a sudden accident or a long lingering illness, the mind slams shut. Reality cannot penetrate the defenses as the mind protects itself. This initial refusal to accept visible truth is an attribute of the mind that is automatic and universal. It is a necessary reflex, like blinking when the eye is confronted with a sudden bright light.

The reflex to slam shut the door to the mind is present in all people, to varying degrees perhaps, but substantially the same. One hears of tragedy and the mind refuses to let the data in, except slowly, through filters like shock and denial, rationalization and unconcern. For some, if the tragedy is not personal, the barriers may never come down.

This is where the difference between a bereaved parent and a co-worker or neighbor becomes obvious. Only the parent lives with the tragedy long enough to let the reality of the horror come fully into the mind, past the barriers of protection. Others go on to other things, still protected by the barriers.

It is natural that the rest of the world protects itself from all of the horror of the world. Otherwise, everyone would be insane from all the tragedy. Worse, they would be numb or callused, and unconcerned.

Fran saw the violence that hit Marlys. Jack learned about it soon, and others learned of it not much later. Everyone's mind slammed shut because the horror was too much to let in. Fran had to deal with it. Marlys is her daughter, and would never be home again, unhurt. Over the days, weeks, and years of healing, the memory is accepted in a place in the mind where it can be looked at, not directly but with perspective.

Marlys wasn't Jack's natural child; she wasn't part of him. These are things that make a parent much more vulnerable, and even though Marlys and Jack were planning a surprise Mother's Day party, he was not vulnerable as is a natural parent. Still, the horror has penetrated his mind, and brings great pain to him.

* * *

People often expect too much of themselves. Many people are tortured by the "if only's" and the "what if's". Anger may be directed at themselves or at others, including family members, one's spouse, the doctors, the person who caused the death, the person who died. Anger is directed at God. Fran says that bereaved parents "are particularly hurt or angry with people who push them into accepting their loss too soon, or who pretend that nothing happened."

After the initial help, relatives and friends usually pick up their own lives and the parent is often left to deal with his or her own grief. Alone. Co-workers, friends, neighbors, and sometimes even family members avoid them or change the subject.

In reality, few people are able to help or to understand as a parent tries to survive the loss of a child. They feel deprived of his or her presence. Shock is nature's way of softening the blow. Shock serves as a cushion, giving the time to absorb the fact of the loss. They hear the words, but they don't comprehend the full impact, not until much later when the friends are gone. Emotions seem frozen when they are in shock.

It takes time to believe what has happened. The denial stage may go on for weeks, or even much longer. Fran looked for Marlys to come home at a regular time. She would see a person that looked like Marlys walking down the street or at a shopping mall. Fran tells of one particularly difficult time. "One day I followed a white Datsun B-210 like Marlys had, because the girl driving it looked just like Marlys. When this car stopped at the Post Office, the reality hit me again, because that was where Marlys would go. It wasn't Marlys, of course."

Fran found she was repeating the same things to the same people. The same thoughts kept running through her head. But, in saying the words, and hearing herself say them over and over again, she began to believe what had happened. It was her way to let the reality break down her own barriers. In a way, even though she saw her in that office in her home, Fran had to persuade herself that it really happened.

* * *

Time slowly begins to build roadblocks on the paths after a loved one dies, safeguards to keep the happiness safe and keep out the pain. So much time is needed. What is the difference between parents and others? Why do parents and loved ones take so long to heal from grief that is, in fact, just as unacceptable to the mind of mere acquaintances or even strangers? Why are some persons impatient for the grieving parent to get on with life, and why do some seem so insensitive toward those still obviously in pain? Is there any hope for those who do not understand the pain of grief? Who has the right to even ask that they understand?

These questions need to be looked at, not to understand the callousness of a friend, but to have the bereaved parents learn to cope with the insensitivity of others and not be hurt more by the lack of care and concern in others. Those who have been hurt by tragedy have to protect themselves from those who just don't understand. More than that, there is a need to open the eyes of those who no longer try to understand with compassion, who no longer have time for the suffering of those who are afflicted.

Consider the words of Paul in Second Corinthians 1:8-10:

> *"For we do not want you to be ignorant, brethren, of the affliction we experienced in Asia; for we were so utterly, unbearably crushed that we despaired of life itself. Why, we felt that we had received the sentence of death; but that was to make us rely not on ourselves but on God who raises the dead; he delivered us from so deadly a*

peril, and he will deliver us; on him we have set our hope that he will deliver us again."

This is the kind of message a bereaved parent will send, saying that we don't want you to be ignorant of the *"affliction we experienced in Minnesota; for we were so utterly, unbearably crushed that we despaired of life itself."* Perhaps Paul survived an attack on his own person, but in those days of the early Christian church, and in those same days of the Jewish church, there were many, many mothers and fathers whose children died, violently. Paul was aware of these grieving parents.

The pain Fran and her family has endured because Marlys was murdered, and the pain others they know have endured because their son or daughter died, is enough so that all bereaved parents can, like Paul, claim that they were *"so utterly, unbearably crushed that we despaired of life itself."*

This is reality, and from this reality they have a right to ask for the same comfort that Paul received. They understand the pain of those in both the New Testament and in the Hebrew Scriptures. What they don't understand as easily is how God delivered them from their unbearable pain. It is time to look to God for some answers.

5

LOOKING TO GOD FOR ANSWERS

A pastor, priest, rabbi or friend might already have consoled the family of the deceased, and perhaps read prayers or Scripture. In many cases, however, the memorial service or funeral is often the first time that "religious words" are spoken. The intention is to bring the word of God to those present and in mourning.

The focus of a religious service on words that promise comfort, invoking God's words and name, raises certain expectations that the words will, in fact, be comfort for the bereaved. Depending upon the religious background and affiliation of the mourners, the words will be familiar words that have been heard and even memorized, or they will be strange words with new thoughts and ideas.

In the one case, for those who have an extensive religious background, old promises of Scripture will be remembered. For those whose background is not in the church, new

27

promises of Scripture will be heard. In both cases, the mourner will hear words that give rise to certain expectations. This is the time when people say, "If I ever needed God, I need God now!"

It is at this time that Scripture is read with the intention of bringing God's word to those present. Words are spoken which illustrate the legitimate expectation of people seeking comfort from God. My loved one has died and I seek comfort now. One looks directly into the eyes of the speaker and hears, *"Thy rod and thy staff shall comfort me."*

* * *

There was a viewing at the funeral home for Marlys, and the long line of friends and relatives extended outside the mortuary because it was so long. The casket was closed, because of her injuries. Her high school senior picture was in a frame placed on top of her casket.

The death of a high school senior just weeks before graduation brings trauma to the whole community and many people came to offer consolation. Fran still has the guest register, of course, and she is amazed to see the names of those who came to pay respects and visit. She doesn't remember much of what happened. It seemed that picking the hymns for the funeral was very important, and she still remembers which ones she selected. The hymns were selected to comfort her, and they have become a reminder of that comfort.

The viewing is a time when the individual comfort of others is extended to the bereaved. Everyone who comes bears his or her own grief to some degree, and they extend sympathies to the family and closest friends. At the viewing for Marlys, the young people were so kind to Fran.

Fran says, "I remember all the kids who spoke to me, even now, so many years later. I remember those who had a kind word. I have a memory of someone kneeling at my feet, crying. I think it may have been one who we suspected was involved in the murder, but I can't be sure that it was him." Fran doesn't know if this young man is guilty or innocent. In some minds, he is still a suspect. But the memory of who knelt and cried is fading while the memory of those who had kind words still is clear.

Fran says, "I don't remember much more. Lots of people were there, and I don't remember them. I remember sitting, and speaking with people. I remember going through the motions. I had to see these people but I didn't want to see them. The doctor had given me a mild sedative. They were the most horrible days of my life."

The funeral was in the morning, on Saturday. There was a procession, by car, from the funeral home in Stillwater to the little church on the hill in Afton. Cars following in the funeral procession were in a line that seemed to have no end as they drove along the St. Croix River that Marlys loved. Fran remembers the line of cars. Jack says it rained.

The funeral service was led by Marlys and Fran's pastor, the Reverend Richard Borgstrom. The service gave opportunity to those who wanted to speak. A poem was read that Fran's daughter, Lynn, then age 16, wrote the night Marlys died. It is at the front of this book.

Pastor Borgstrom delivered a message of comfort, based upon Scripture, and offered comfort to the family and friends who had packed the church to overflowing. He spoke clearly of the comfort offered and of the promise of victory over death in Jesus Christ. His words spoke of the joy that Marlys has in being with God. He also spoke of the comfort that God offered to those who mourn.

To his credit, Pastor Borgstrom also spoke of the inability to find words that justify the murder of Marlys, and the inability to find words that justify or explain much of the evil in the world. He didn't have all the answers, but he offered God as a comfort.

After the funeral service, the casket was lowered into the grave at the cemetery, next to the church. More prayers were spoken. Fran says, "I looked to God for comfort, starting with the church service, I guess, and I continue to look for comfort from God. I have found that comfort, over the years, and my faith in God is stronger now than ever."

* * *

Reality comes into people's lives, violently and with finality, so that they can no longer hold on to abstract idealism about how life should be. Promises are no longer enough in the face of violent reality, unless one can see how these promises are going to be kept. Grief from the loss of a child brings unbearable pain, and the words of Scripture do not ease that pain.

Even if one can concentrate on the written words, it is so hard to apply them to this reality. Often, reality intrudes in a life, or a family or a nation in such a way that words of God do not comfort sufficiently. Reality sometimes is so powerful that one seeks more than comfort. One asks God for answers. One asks God for answers when one hears the anguished cry, "God, why did you let this happen? Why didn't you do something? God?"

To deny this legitimate crying out for answers is to hide from that reality and to

31

prevent any possible recovery based upon faith. It is essential to ask God for answers. Those who ask God for answers, and who do not expect simple answers to very complicated questions, will find answers to those questions. Scripture promises comfort and it also promises answers to the hard questions. To do otherwise is to ignore God. Worse, to do otherwise is to deny one's self the opportunity to have answers so that one can be healed.

At a funeral, when Scripture is read or sermons are preached and prayers prayed, it is understood that the one who has died is no longer being comforted. Marlys's service was intended to celebrate her return to the Lord whom she loved and in whom she believed. The service was to remember her.

The funeral service was also for those who are left behind. It was to allow the opportunity to those who are left with the reality of life after a loved one has died to honor the loved one, pay respects to one who has died, and to mourn. Marlys's service was for Fran and the family and friends who gathered in that little white church on the hill, asking for comfort, and looking to God for answers.

* * *

At a memorial service for a woman who had lived over ninety years of good Christian living, who was loved and missed by hundreds of family and friends, a pastor spoke with joy about her victory in Christ. Another pastor spoke to give comfort to the family, to say that it was appropriate to mourn the loss at the same time that the victory is celebrated.

For those who mourn, especially for those who mourn the death of a child, grief is a reality that must be faced. Their pain is so real that it must be understood. Their expectations that their child would survive them is so strong that those persons, above all, should look to God for answers.

At a memorial service, Scripture is read as a comfort to those who remain. One very popular Scripture is from John 14:2-3, which says:

"In my Father's house are many rooms; if it were not so, would I have told you that I go to prepare a place for you? And when I go and prepare a place for you, I will come again and will take you to myself, that where I am you may be also."

As one reads that text, and as one looks into the eyes of the bereaved, one sees the parent say, "Yes, my loved one is with Jesus, even now, but why does it hurt so much?"

What about the pain the parents suffer now, here at the funeral and for days, weeks, years after? Isn't it a reasonable expectation that Scripture will give words of comfort, words that will ease the pain, even take it away?

Expectations that a good life like Marlys lived will be rewarded may somehow be fulfilled in heaven. Expectations of comfort are contradicted, however, by the death of the child or spouse, or by starvation in Ethiopia, or death squads in El Salvador, or Jesus on the cross. Marlys's death was outside reasonable expectations.

Genesis 1:31 says:

"And God saw everything that he had made, and behold, it was very good."

How can what we experience be good? Parents ask, "How, God, am I comforted by you going to prepare rooms for us? How does that take away my pain, even if Marlys is in one of those rooms? Is it so much nicer than the room I gave her?"

6

OF THE SAME MIND AS CHRIST

In the pain of the loss of a child, deep felt grief leads to difficult questions. What is fair, and why is evil? How could God allow this to happen? What did I do to cause, or even deserve this pain? Why did it have to be my child? These are some of the questions that are asked of God by parents who are experiencing pain that is unbearable. This book presents an answer to these questions.

To understand the answer that this book offers, we believe it is necessary to look to God for that answer. We have found that it is necessary to believe in God when the hard questions are asked of God. Even if one is filled with anger or pain or depression, the first step is to admit that God exists. If the grieving parent, out of anger or pain or depression, denies that God exists it will not be possible to ask the questions that need to be asked. Life then becomes meaningless, and so does the death of the child.

Only if God can be called upon for answers does life after the death of a child have any meaning. And only then when God is called upon for answers does the life of the child have any meaning. In so many words, a person can only begin to make sense out of the death of a child when that person is willing to look to God for that answer. Said another way, without God there is no sense to what has happened. With God, at the very least, there is some place to go to ask the questions. This is why one is to look to God for answers.

How does one look to God for answers when it is hard even to feel God's presence in the midst of grief? This is done, not by any special words, but through understanding the life and humanity of Jesus Christ, and the comfort of the Holy Spirit. It is not much easier for persons who already have strong faith to seek answers than it is for one with little or no faith. It may even be easier to cry out to God, asking, even demanding to know why a child has died.

Yet out of an affirmation that the child who has died did not live without meaning and did not die a meaningless death, comes the affirmation that God provides an answer. A child has meaning for the parents. All that is left of the child are the memories and the promise that life has meaning. The parents themselves want to understand that meaning. To find this meaning, it is important to look to the life of Jesus Christ, and the meaning that Christ's life has for today.

*   *   *

What is this understanding of Jesus Christ? Are there words that summarize this life and humanity? There are words in Philippians 2:1-8 which Paul wrote as an understanding of the source of answers from the life of Jesus Christ:

> *So if there is any encouragement in Christ, any incentive of love, any participation in the Spirit, any affection and sympathy, complete my joy by being of the same mind, having the same love, being in full accord and of one mind. Do nothing from selfishness or conceit, but in humility count others better than yourselves. Let each of you look not to his own interests, but also to the interests of others. Have this in mind among yourselves, which is yours in Christ Jesus, who, though he was in the form of God, did not count equality with God a thing to be grasped, but emptied himself, taking the form of a servant being born in the likeness of men. And being found in human form he humbled himself and became obedient unto death, even death on a cross.*

This Scripture offers the expectation that good feelings come from being "of the same mind" as Christ. It gives the admonishment to look to the interests of others, and not just our own. Jesus Christ is held up as an example, as he became human, and in human form suffered death on a cross. Jesus gave his life because he humbled himself, and was obedient. We also are to humble ourselves and be obedient.

This is the answer that a bereaved parent receives as he or she struggles with the pain and grief of the death of their child. The parent is admonished to look to the others. The parent is told that it is necessary to be humble, and even to die.

What does this mean? How can obedience and humility be of value at a time like this? What kind of answer is this? As we continue to live, with our pain and our loss and our grief, are we comforted by an understanding of the life and humanity of Jesus Christ? Are we to die too?

The first part of the answer to these questions is yes. We must be willing to die in order to have comfort in our pain. The other part of the answer is that we are not to die for ourselves, because there is no obedience or humility in that. Instead, we must be willing to die for others. We will lose our pain to the extent that we live for others.

The answer to our pain is that we need to understand that our pain is unbearable to us initially, but that others have borne that pain, and others will bear that pain after us.

This understanding comes from a merger of two parts of the way that suffering is seen. It is intellectual, viewing suffering and pain from without, as an observer. And it is also existential, viewing suffering and pain from within, as a participant. When we can see that others have the pain that we have experienced, we seek to comfort them. When we seek to comfort them, we are comforted.

*   *   *

Fran has found a poem that says it another way. The poem has been reprinted here as a summary of the struggle for healing and the discovery that healing can take place. The poem was found by Fran in a newsletter of one of The Compassionate Friends, Inc. chapters.

The author is Barbara Williams, of Fort Wayne, Indiana. Barbara is a Licensed Professional Nurse, working in an Emergency room of a hospital. She wrote the poem late at night after a long conversation with a bereaved parent. Barbara is also a bereaved parent and dedicates the poem to the memory of her daughter Dawn (1976) and son Randy (1978) and also to her living children Linda, Cyndi, John, Vincent, and Krissi. She says that the love, patience and understanding of her living children helped her cross the "Stepping Stones."

The comfort that the poem gives, and the understanding of the feelings of a bereaved parent are so right that it is certain that the author is also one who grieves and one who has experienced healing.

STEPPING STONES
by
Barbara Williams

Come, take my hand, the road is long. We must travel by stepping stones. No, you're not alone. I'll go with you. I know the road well, I've been there. Don't fear the darkness. I'll be with you. We must take one step at a time. But remember we may have to stop a while. It is a long way to the other side and there are many obstacles.
We have many stones to cross. Some are bigger than others...SHOCK, DENIAL and ANGER to start. Then comes GUILT, DESPAIR and LONELINESS. It's a hard road to travel but it must be done. It's the only way to reach the other side.
Come, slip your hand in mine. What? Oh yes, it's strong. I've held so many hands like yours. Yes, mine was

one time small and weak like yours.
Once, you see, I had to take someone's
hand in order to take the first step.
Oops! you've stumbled. Go ahead and
cry. Don't be ashamed, I understand.
Let's wait here a while and get your
breath. When you're stronger we'll go
on, one step at a time. There's no need
to hurry.

    Say, it's nice to hear you laugh.
Yes, I agree, the memories you shared
are good. Look, we're half way there
now; I can see the other side. It looks
so warm and sunny. Oh, have you
noticed? We're nearing the last stone
and, you're standing alone. And look,
your hands, you've let go of mine, and
we've reached the other side.

    But wait. Look back. Someone is
standing there. They are alone and
want to cross the stepping stones. I
better go; they need my help. What?
Are you sure? Why yes; I'll wait. You
know the way - you've been there. Yes,
I agree - it's your turn, my friend - to
help someone else across the stepping
stones.

This poem beautifully speaks about
helping others cross to the other side, across
stepping stones like denial, despair and
loneliness, and ends with the desire to help
another, rather than being helped. This is the
answer, said another way. It is not until the

bereaved think of others more than themselves that they begin to heal.

More will be said about this later, but the key words are "others more than ourselves." When the bereaved respond to God's call to love others as themselves, when Fran responded to God's call to love others who needed help on the stepping stones, they and she began to heal. This merger of being healed and healing others is the answer that comes from looking to God for answers.

* * *

At some memorial services, the message may be concluded with a call to conversion. The speaker issues what is known as an altar call by asking for conversion. Those who have heard the message are asked to come forward, to repent, to accept God, to change, to surrender one's self to God. When it is expected, it is appropriate and may, in fact, help some of those in attendance.

In other settings, where such a call is not regularly part of the worship style, it may not be appropriate. Still, pastors and priests will say that the funeral or memorial service is the only time they have to reach many in attendance, who do not go to church and who do not believe in God. They structure their remarks for those people, at least in part. Those priests and pastors who dare to ask

42

God for answers also ask those at the service to recognize that there is a God to whom questions can be put. This is sometimes the first small seed of hope.

But how does this help the bereaved parent? How is this an answer if the mother of the child has her faith? What about the conflict between expectation, of comfort, and experience, of pain? The answer, as we have said, isn't found in a few words but in the merger of our pain with the pain of others, in the life and humanity of Jesus Christ.

Christ, in his life on earth took many years to live and give us that example. Any healing that is said to be immediate is contrary to the expectations of many and to the experiences of everyone. The stepping stones are long. It is not until we can help others that we are helped in our pain.

How long until we are helped? How long has it taken to even remember that there are others?

7

THEY DID NOT KNOW WHAT TO SAY

At first, amid the shock and pain, persons who are in the early stages of grief hardly notice others who are around them. They hardly remember who was at the funeral or memorial service. They forget who brought a meal to feed the rest of the family.

Many people run away from bereaved people and try to avoid contact with them, even when they are aware of a responsibility to help those suffering from a loss of a child. Ministers, rabbis and priests stay away because they know the bereaved is in pain and they don't know what to say to them. The clergy are aware of times when they have tried to say something and it was the wrong thing. Every clergy and counselor has stories of saying the wrong thing.

Estimates by grief-related organizations suggest that a large number of parents who lose a child drop out of church. The largest single reason is the minister, rabbi or priest. If professionals make these mistakes, so do friends and relatives and acquaintances, saying the wrong thing, meaning well. The second largest cause of these parents dropping out of church is the congregation. They offer no oil of joy for mourning, because they too do not know what to say.

Often, when relationships are ongoing, pain and hurt build up and greater stress occurs instead of healing. Grief-related organizations have also found that many of the parents of children who have died get a divorce in the first few years after the loss. Some spouses claim that the divorce was going to happen anyway, but often this is rationalization, transferring pain and its cause to one's mate.

Sometimes, this pain is also transferred to other children or to one's own parents or in-laws. The tragedy of all this transfer of anger is that it could be prevented, or at least limited. If only people would talk together, and try to express how they feel, perhaps they would not make the pain worse. Perhaps the time they spend together will be healing instead of harmful. But, they ask, what can I do when I am in so much pain, and no one really wants to listen to me?

It is fair to want to know what to say to those who are in such great pain. It is fair for them to want to know why no one will talk with them. It is important that people talk during the early time of grief, and so it is important to find out what to say to them.

*   *   *

Much of the destructive conduct that damages or ruins relationships can be prevented. There are two general rules or guidelines to keep in mind at all times. Whether one is clergy or spouse or friend, there are two things to remember. First, it is important to listen to the bereaved, listen long after you think that no more needs to be said. Second, if you have to talk, don't say the wrong thing.

Talking with a bereaved parent is difficult sometimes, so that the first recommendation, listening to the parent long after you think there is no more that needs to be said, will be hard. But it is necessary if you are going to help them recover. People who suppress their grief are often in a continual state of stress and shock. They are unable to move beyond that state. Grief that stays locked up inside a person can actually change that person, and even destroy that person, as a poison does that is not taken out of the system.

Grieving people have physical effects from the shock and trauma of the death of a loved one. The stress comes out in high blood pressure, ulcers, cancer and many other body ailments. It is important to be able help these suffering people so they will not destroy their bodies, their marriages, their careers. In Fran's early stages of grief, her body went through a lot of very, very bad changes. She had paralysis, shortness of breath, and pains and, as she says, "I had just about everything you could imagine, and at times I thought I was going crazy."

Fran has found that her experiences are quite common. She was left with a sense of unreality. She had a strong sense of guilt as a survivor. Events were complicated by involvement with medical and legal authorities. Her need to blame someone was extremely strong, particularly since the murder has not been solved. She was left with a sense of helplessness, and at times exhibited high levels of agitation. She, like so many bereaved parents, has regrets for things not said or activities not done with Marlys. To this day, she struggles with trying to understand why Marlys was murdered.

All these feelings are very common and are experienced by almost everyone at one time or another. Sometimes, the terrible feelings and the stress overshadow the fact that there is a real need to talk and be talked with. It is important for those who would offer comfort to be physically present as well as to be emotionally supportive.

The overriding principle of grief ministry is just simply being there for the bereaved. It is so important not to allow your grieving friend to remain isolated. Remember that you can reach out to this person even though you cannot take away the pain. You can help him to tolerate what he is going through. Let your genuine concern and caring for her show. Try gently to plant the seeds of hope that some day the pain will decrease, and listen without being judgmental.

The bereaved parent may not be able to say clearly what he or she wants in the way of support. This does not mean, however, that the bereaved do not have certain very real, even strong expectations. Studies show that the bereaved want others to comfort them, particularly others who have been there and really understand. But even those who don't have an experience of this magnitude to draw on can respond to the expectations of the grieving person by being present, and by listening.

It is good to allow the bereaved to cry, and even encourage them to continue crying if they show signs of starting to cry. They expect you to understand that they have a need to cry, and that they are adult and mature and adjusted, but this is too much to bear alone.

Let the bereaved friend or family member talk and tell the story, over and over and over. Do not be amazed if the griever talks about many of the same things over and over. They expect to be able to express their feelings and will be hurt if you do not let them do so. Both you and they will find confidence in knowing that talking, and repeating, is normal.

This is all part of the healing process. Fortunately, Pastor Borgstrom, told Jack at the funeral that he would have to listen and listen, and that he should always appear to be interested in hearing the story again. Many times, he had to remember those words, but, yes, sometimes he forgot.

* * *

Parents expect you to mention the dead child's name often when talking with them. This is very important. We encourage the griever to realistically review and talk about the deceased and their mutual relationship. Be a long term listener, not just on the first day or the first week, but in the weeks and months to follow.

If you start to listen, you will be expected to continue listening. You are not expected to have the answer as long as you continue to listen. Even after a year, do not be afraid of your silence and listening as you talk with the bereaved person. You are expected to listen and be there, and if the bereaved is important enough to you to begin a relationship, he or she is important enough to continue it.

Above all, let them set the time schedule for healing. Unless you have been there, you just will not know how long it takes. If you have been there, you know that it takes forever, but there are stages of healing. Let each person walk that journey at his or her own pace, crossing the stepping stones at their pace. And remember to be there with them, offering the hand they need.

* * *

This principle of being there is fundamental to what we have called the theology of accompaniment. There is a passage in the Gospel of Mark which describes this principle in action. It takes place during the time just before Jesus is taken to his death on the cross, in the Garden of Gethsemane.

From this text, it is clear that even the closest friends of Jesus did not understand what was happening, and moreover, they did not know what to do or say. This text demonstrates some of the problems that are found by all who seek to comfort one who is suffering in a way and because of some reason which he or she just does not understand.
Mark 14:32-40 says:

And they went to a place which was

called Gethsemane; and he said to his disciples, "Sit here, while I pray." And he took with him Peter and James and John, and began to be greatly distressed and troubled. And he said to them, "My soul is very sorrowful, even to death; remain here, and watch." And going a little farther, he fell on the ground and prayed that, if it were possible, the hour might pass from him. And he said, "Abba, Father, all things are possible to thee; remove this cup from me; yet not what I will, but what thou wilt." And he came and found them sleeping, and he said to Peter, "Simon, are you asleep? Could you not watch one hour? Watch and pray that you may not enter into temptation; the spirit indeed is willing, but the flesh is weak." And again he went away and prayed, saying the same words. And again he came and found them sleeping, for their eyes were very heavy; and they did not know what to say to him."

How many times do well-meaning friends act just like Peter, James and John? Jesus said that he needed them to be there with him. They could not even keep their eyes open. They did not have the energy to support their friend, especially since they didn't even understand why there was so much grief. They did not know what to say to

51

him. Scripture does not record that Peter or James or John tried to say anything. Perhaps they had logical answers and perhaps they said nothing.

In their time of trial, for Peter and John (in Acts 4) or in prison, for James and Peter (in Acts 12) perhaps Gesthemane was repeated. Perhaps having been there as Jesus asked for accompaniment helped them. Most likely, they expected others to be there with them and to listen even if they had nothing to say.

Grieving parents find that they want and expect others to be with them. They want to talk about what has happened. Their expectations can be met, but only when we are present, with them in accompaniment. And those who sit with the bereaved need just as much as Peter, James and John to learn what to say at such a time.

For the most part, talking with the bereaved is a process of accompaniment, of being there. Those who genuinely want to help are trying not to fall asleep in the garden of Gesthemane or at the kitchen table, hearing the same story over and over, and over again. What can they say?

At first, the grieving person will not even know that others are there. And yet, this presence is the best thing that they can offer. It must be remembered that at first, the pain is so great that one does not even notice that others are present. Healing is only just beginning when one can recognize the presence of others. Healing is only just starting when some small concern for the interests of others breaks into the pain-shrouded emotional paralysis which has been gripping emotions like a vice.

One notices that another person is present, in accompaniment, and the pain subsides, just a bit, for just a moment. The presence of another dimly enters the grieving one's mind. He or she is aware that a cup of tea has been placed by her hand at the right time. Someone has picked up the other children from school. She wonders who did that act of kindness. A faucet that drips has been fixed. Even, maybe, the grass has been cut. He wonders who has been so nice.

The one trying to reach the bereaved has not performed any magical act. He or she was just there, doing something that they think their loved one will need, will notice, and will appreciate. These small acts of love and concern often start the healing.

8

UNLESS YOU SAY THE WRONG THING

During the time of early healing, beginning even at the memorial service or funeral, words are spoken in an attempt to console. Some of the things that are said are not comforting at all. Some things hurt, and others show lack of compassion. If the words are harmless enough, the grieving parent won't remember what was said. In fact, it is a generalization that has been true most every time that those in the deep pain of the death of a child won't remember a thing you say, unless you say the wrong thing.

For the most part, what one says to the bereaved won't even make an impression unless one says the wrong thing. Even if one thinks that these things are true, there is no reason to say them to someone who is in grief from the death of their child. If they are newly bereaved, it will hurt them greatly. If they have begun to recover, you just might get a response that hurts you.

This second part of the guidelines for talking with a bereaved parent is also built on the theology of accompaniment, of being there with the person in pain. The reason why one takes the time to sit with one in pain, and the reason why one seeks to comfort him or her is, and has to be, founded on love. It may not be love of spouse or parent or friend, but it, at least, must be Christian love.

The professional clergy, the priests and pastors speak of love for their flock. Certainly friends and family should show love above all else. It is not time to give answers, especially answers that purport to explain why or how a horrible event like the death of a child occurs. But it is a time of love, of accompaniment, and not of easy answers. Words that are spoken at this time must be based on love, and not knowledge. At this time in the bereaved's healing, nothing is as important as love, and so the words must convey that love.

Love and particularly Christian love are words which might have different meanings for different people. What is meant here, and what is needed by the bereaved who are in so much pain, is unconditional love that is based upon compassion and not on understanding. This is the meaning behind the words of Paul in First Corinthians 13: 1-2, which say:

If I speak in the tongues of men and of angels, but have not love, I am a noisy gong or a clanging cymbal. And if I have prophetic powers, and understand all mysteries and all knowledge, and if I have all faith, so as to remove mountains, but have not love, I am nothing.

Everything that is said should be governed by this concept, that this is not the time for answers but is the time for love. Love is the foundation of accompaniment, and it is the guiding light that prevents us from sounding like a noisy gong or clanging cymbal. Love keeps us from saying the wrong thing.

* * *

Have you heard someone say, "God wanted your child more than you did?" Are they kidding? This is the voice of a clanging cymbal. The bereaved parent knows that God has eternity to have my child, after I have a chance to raise my child to maturity and my child/adult can live a good life. God can wait.

No matter the theological assumption upon which such a statement might be based, it is not love to presume to know how much God wanted a child and, by saying that, actually deny how much the parent also wanted that child.

*   *   *

Have you heard someone say, "You'll get over it in a few weeks." Studies show that the pain of grief from loss of a child is almost as strong on the first anniversary of the death as it is at the time of death. On the annivarsary, there is no shock for protection, and the reality is becoming clearly final. And that is just the first year. No more can the parent say, "Last year, my child and I were together at this time. Last year, we did this together."

In reality, who can say when another should be healed, or even be healing? Unless one has experienced the death of his or her own child, there is no idea how long it takes to get over it. If she has had the experience, she knows it takes forever to be completely recovered, and that a person is lucky if she is healing in the first year.

*   *   *

Have you heard someone say, "You have (or can have) other children." Each child, each individual is unique. Shared memories and emotions cannot be transferred like title to property. Each child is part of the parent, and one is not consoled over losing one part of herself by the fact that she may have another part.

Each child has the right to grow up in a loving relationship with his or her parents, even though that may not be the reality that the child experiences. It is unreasonable to ask a parent or child to be a substitute for another. This denies the individuality of the child who has died. Not only does this place a burden on the remaining children to become someone they cannot be, it prevents the parents and children from helping each other in their grief.

*   *   *

Have you heard someone say, "God is punishing you for something." Not only is this cruel, placing guilt on an already vulnerable person, this is saying that a child can be allowed to die as punishment for the sins of another. This totally trivializes the life of the child just at the time when the parents are seeking to find meaning in their child's death.

Not only is such a statement lacking in love, it is theologically arrogant to know what God would decide to do about a sin in the face of so much sin in the world. Of course, saying that God is punishing the child for some sin is no better as a comfort or as a theological position. It is best not to talk about sin in such a situation unless you are God or unless you are sinless.

*   *   *

Have you heard someone say, "Your child is better off with Jesus." While it is true that being in the presence of God is wonderful, it is not love to suggest that the parent is not the natural and proper place for the child to be. Notice that the speaker does not volunteer his or her child to be with God at an age that is not natural.

How do you respond when the parent asks, "What kind of parent does that make me, that I can't make life nice enough for my child?" All bereaved parents we have ever met say that their child is with God. That doesn't stop the pain of their loss.

* * *

Have you been tempted to say, "We are only given what we can handle." The first calm reaction to that is to ask, "If I were weaker, would my child still be alive? If I am stronger, will God take my other children too?"

Many times words like these are spoken as the parent is on the verge of collapse, either emotionally or physically. How does this give strength to continue, when to collapse might bring back her child?

* * *

Have you been tempted to say, "God has a plan." Many people believe that God is in control of every event in every life. If the parent believes that, she or he has probably thought of that. If they don't believe that there is a plan, or aren't sure, now is not the time to get out the blueprint.

They are not interested in knowing that God planned this grief, this pain that is the worst news, the worst event in their life. Most, if not all, grieving parents would rather have died than have their child die. They will not find God or comfort in plans. You will be lucky if they only tell you that "It is time for plan B."

* * *

There is another text from the Bible that is often used at times of grief. It is more often than not misquoted or misunderstood. It is a source of confusion because it is not carefully read, and assumptions are made which are not based on what is written.

Paul's first letter to the Thessalonians 5: 16-18, says:

"Rejoice always, pray constantly, give thanks in all circumstances; for this is the will of God in Christ Jesus for you."

This text is misread, especially the phrase, "give thanks FOR all circumstances;" when the language is "give thanks IN all circumstances." People are not exhorted by this Scripture to give thanks for the fact that their child has died. Rather, and most importantly, they are urged to give thanks to God in these times of grief. They don't thank God for the death of their child, but they may thank God for the comfort they receive in their grief, if others don't say the wrong thing.

Secondly, it is important to see that the language which says "this is the will of God" refers to the "rejoicing," the "praying," the "giving thanks IN all," and does not refer to the specific events, particularly the death of a child. The wrong thing should not be said. If what you are about to say to someone in grief offers easy or simple answers, don't say it. There are no easy answers, there is only accompaniment.

The two things which need to be remembered, as one actively seeks to comfort or be comforted, are not difficult to remember. First, the person who needs to talk is the person experiencing the grief. Second, the person who is interested in helping should offer love, not advice or opinions.

Especially in the early stages of grief, all that can be said and all that can be heard is, "I'm sorry," and if you have been there yourself, you can say "I understand." If you have not been there, all you can add is, "I'm here for you."

9

ANGER AND UNDERSTANDING

During the time Marlys was at the hospital, before the certainty of her death was accepted as fact, anger was experienced for the first time. Between Tuesday afternoon, when the ambulance arrived, and Thursday evening, when the arrangements were complete for Marlys to be an organ donor, all who were directly involved were angry at least once, as their very souls cried out in pain.

At the hospital, Fran was given a mild sedative and all of the extended family was called. Fran's son, Raymond, who is two years older than Marlys, was one of the first to arrive. Ray's anger at the unknown assailant, the murderer, and Ray's frustration at not knowing who to be angry with, was great. Several times, he was heard to shout, "It's my sister who is in there. Why can't I have an answer?"

For a twenty year old man, it was a hard way to take the last steps of growing up. It was a hard way for him to have to face death. Ray was like all young people, tending to believe that if they are not immortal, at least they are going to live forever. Ray, like most people his age, had not seen death, except for very old relatives. Ray, like most people, like all the rest of us, had been shocked by the violence, and he was angry.

He said, "I'll kill the one who did it." In this he was joined by most of the friends and family who gathered at the hospital. Striking back at the one who caused all this pain is normal and Ray did as well as any young man with his anger. After all, his father and his maternal grandmother also said, "I'll kill the one who did it." No one does much better in coping with that thing that cannot be understood. Death.

* * *

Before all of the family was able to arrive at the hospital, the first of several misunderstandings occurred. In little ways, the anger built. Who should call this relative? Who should be allowed to talk with the doctors? Who is the one who is hurt most? Who is in charge, and is that person responsible? And most awful, where were you when it happened?

In the lack of knowledge about who could have committed the murder, anger led to suspicion. Why else would someone say, "I don't care who did it, I'll kill the murderer!"

Everyone whose child dies has great anger that somehow must be dealt with if peace is to come. In the case where the cause is known, such as in auto accidents or illness or violence where the perpetrator is known, the anger can be directed at the specific individual. Even when the doctor did the best job that modern medicine can provide, there is anger. Even when the driver was not drunk, and had no way to prevent the accident, there is anger.

When our child commits suicide, dies by his or her own hand, that anger will be directed at the child. A father we know whose daughter took her own life with a gun she had secretly purchased talks about how he screamed at her when he found her, dying from the self-inflicted gunshot wound. There is anger.

More than 11 years after the murder, the thought of killing the one responsible for Marlys's murder is no longer said. Still, it is deep in everyone's private thoughts and has to be brought out into the open. Marlys's family is unable to vent their anger at the drunken driver, or the careless doctor, or at anyone specific in name. But they still need to deal with the anger that is there.

For some of the family, it feels good to be angry at one person or another. For others in the family, the anger has somehow been eased. Forgiveness has been granted to the killer, or, at least, the effort to forgive has been made. Some of them no longer dwell on the emotional fuel of revenge, directed at real or imagined persons.

When the murder is solved, if it is, the anger will rage once again, more angry than at the time Marlys was killed. When the murderer is found, no matter what we have done until now, there will be anger. Someone again will say, "I'll kill that person." We pray that no one will actually try to kill that person. We know this, however. There will be anger.

* * *

One of the things that grief counselors say is that it is all right to be angry. Anger is a natural emotion, a natural response to death and, of course, the counselors are not giving permission to experience what is a natural reaction. They know it is necessary to have an outlet for the anger in order to return to a semblance of normality.

The permission that is given is to express the anger, to vent it, as it were, so that it does not dwell inside, causing physical and emotional damage. The hurt of the loss, and the pain, will always be with the bereaved parent. Anger is there, but it needs to be dealt with if there is going to be healing.

If anger is not dealt with, it will cause more pain. The anger has to be expressed, and those who are around the grieving parent will hopefully understand that the anger comes and has to come out. Other bereaved parents know this. Those who have not been there most often do not understand, and so they do not know what to say. We hope that they will remember to say, "I'm here for you."

* * *

Many times, as the pain of the loss increases, as the protective layers of shock wear off, anger comes out that is directed toward those who are not responsible for the illness or accident or other tragedy that took the child unfairly from them. This is why, as has been noted, many marriages in which a child dies end in divorce.

Each partner blames the other, because neither can blame himself. A way to forgive the unforgivable, even when there is no blame, has not been found. There is so much pain, and the anger is there. It is too late to understand, and even when one partner does understand, there often is not enough energy to care.

Many times, anger is directed at surviving children, both in and outside the family. Why should that child have a good life? My child is dead. There is anger, even when the one who is angry knows it is wrong.

A friend whose son was killed in an auto accident came over to visit Fran. The friend arrived sobbing, in tears, crying, unable to unbuckle her seat belt. A neighbor had brought her son over to ask if they knew how to tie a bow tie for a tuxedo. It was prom weekend, five years after her son Jon was killed.

The neighbor meant no harm. She was a good friend and remembered that Jon's parents go to formal affairs. Surely they could help. Jon's mother tied the tie, smiling all the while. She sent the neighbors on their way and drove over to Fran's house. The crying started before she arrived, as did the need to speak out in anger at an unfair life.. That is the kind of anger that the bereaved understand.

10

EVEN ANGRY WITH GOD

Sooner or later, regardless of the religious faith of the person, there is anger at God. People rage at God. They say, "After all, if God is so powerful, how can God let this happen to my child?" Other people also rage at God. They say, "After all, if God is so good, how can God let this happen to my child?"

This conflict with our understanding of God has led some to abandon hope in God. Rabbi Harold S. Kushner has struggled with this conflict in his book, *When Bad Things Happen To Good People*, and has resolved it in his own mind. Rabbi Kushner describes his choice between an all-powerful God and a loving God, and decides on a God of love. Kushner argues that if God is all powerful, God could have prevented the death of Kushner's child. If God is a loving God, then God feels the pain that Kushner feels. Kushner would rather have a God who is sympathetic than one who could prevent bad things and doesn't do so.

Many people make a similar choice if they don't abandon belief in God altogether. When the experiences of reality do not coincide with the expectations of people seeking comfort, how can there be understanding? How can they surrender themselves to God if this God is either all powerful or all loving? Isn't it our experience that God is not both? If God is not both, who can worship a God that could have saved our child? Who needs a loving God that can't bring back our dead child?

The answer to these questions is not found in intellectual arguments, of course, but in the merger of one's pain with the pain of others, in the life and humanity of Jesus Christ. The help does not come from knowing that God is all powerful or that God is all loving. This understanding comes from the experience of helping others, of being present for others, eventually of being willing to give one's own life for others.

* * *

One time Jack had the opportunity to meet a world famous religious leader, Dr. Emilio Castro, General Secretary of the World Council of Churches. Rather than ask him about his work, Jack presumed that the need to understand grief theologically was more important. "How," he asked him, "do you as a pastor deal with death, particularly the death of a child?"

Dr. Castro was gracious in his response. He responded, "I have no answers. I hope that the family who I go to visit is not home, that they will not open their door to me. Because they are home and let me in, I sit and listen, as they talk about how they feel."

That evening, Jack told this story to bereaved parents. They didn't care who it was that had talked with Jack. But when they heard what the person had said, there was an amazing flood of agreement and vitality. "Yes," they said, almost as a group, "being there is the only help."

In their suffering, bereaved parents have experienced that being there is the helping gesture that is needed. They have also come to reject any answers that do not include that understanding.

* * *

Those who were with Jesus in the Garden of Gethsemane did not know what to say to him. Once again, in Mark 14:36, Jesus acknowledges that God is all powerful and all loving, saying,

> *"Abba, Father, all things are possible to thee; remove this cup from me; yet not what I will, but what thou wilt."*

70

Seminary Professor Dorothee Soelle has commented on this part of the life of Jesus Christ in her book, *Suffering,* where she looks at the Gethsemane experience. At page 79, Dr. Soelle writes, "Thus Jesus prayed that he would be spared the agony that lay before him. But to this plea he receives no answer. God is silent, as he has been so often in the history of mankind, and Jesus remains alone with his repeated cry, his fear of death, his insane hope, his threatened life." At page 81, Dr. Soelle continues, "In Gethsemane, Jesus made two futile attempts: he implored his father to spare him, and he asked people to console him." She adds, "Precisely that makes him one with all people and their indifferent neighbors."

The life and humanity of Jesus Christ is not a sugar-coated earthly version of heaven. Without going into a long description of Jesus' life as we know it from Scripture, we can accept this summary, that it was "one with all people and their indifferent neighbors." Everyone suffers, perhaps not as a bereaved parent, but everyone suffers. Everyone is indifferent to the suffering of one's neighbors, perhaps only because we do not understand the grief of a bereaved parent.

If one takes this interpretation of the life of Jesus, and derives an expectation from it, does it not in fact coincide with one's experience?

Aren't bereaved parents alone? Don't they cry out, "Remove this loss from me?" Do not their friends fall asleep at the kitchen table? Isn't their life one with the life and humanity of Jesus Christ?

Where is the hope? Why shouldn't we be angry with God? Where is some sign that God understands? If now our experience coincides with our expectations, is God all powerful and all loving? Where is the hope we have been promised?

*   *   *

Once again we read Scripture to see what Jesus says about the tragedy that besets us all. The words of Jesus are quoted at Matthew 5:43-45:

> *"You have heard that it was said, 'You shall love your neighbor and hate your enemy.' But I say to you, Love your enemies and pray for those who persecute you, so that you may be sons of your Father who is in heaven; for he makes his sun rise on the evil and on the good, and sends rain on the just and on the unjust."*

Jesus did not ignore the suffering of others, but rather called all people to love both neighbor and enemy. Compassion, like the sun, shines on the evil and the good. Suffering, like rain, falls on the just and the

72

unjust. Jesus is one with all people who suffer, because God sends sun and rain on Jesus and on all people. Jesus calls us to love both neighbor and enemy because Jesus is not one with those who are indifferent neighbors. Their time will come. Just as it came to Peter, James and John, and the others in Gethsemane, It comes to every person.

Hope arises when we realize that our suffering makes us one with the life and humanity of Jesus. It does not bring back our child. We still get angry, even angry with God. But, as we are one in Jesus' life, we get understanding. We realize that God is silent when we cry out in anger, but God is present with us as well. God understands that being there is the only help. In that we find hope.

11

WHEN YOU NOTICE THAT YOU ARE ALONE

At first, the pain that a parent feels when her child dies is so intense that shock functions to protect. The full grief of the loss is not experienced all at once. But as the shock wears off, the pain increases and we seem to get worse rather than better.

Unless a person has had this same experience, he really doesn't understand why the parent isn't beginning to recover. He doesn't understand that grief has driven the bereaved parent into a state of isolation from the rest of the world. The rest of the family ceases to exist as the parent is isolated by grief.

When Marlys was killed, Fran went into shock, just to survive. She was unaware of anyone around her and has little memory of the details of the first few days. Later, she began to notice that she was alone. As the full impact began to break though into her consciousness that Marlys would never be

74

with her again in this life, and that they would no longer be able to talk together, Fran realized that she really was alone with her grief. Even her other children didn't know how alone she was.

* * *

Lynn, Fran's younger daughter, who was then 16 years old, was frightened too. Even before all the family had gathered, during the first few hours after Marlys was taken to the hospital, Lynn had been taken to the home of a friend. When we talked to her on the phone, before Marlys had been brought down from surgery, Lynn said she didn't want to come to the hospital. Although Jack had no authority to do so, he told her she had to come to the hospital. She could bring a friend if she wanted, but she had to be at the hospital. Fran and Lynn, and Lynn's good friend ended up staying in a nearby hotel until the other arrangements were made.

Lynn, in her inexperience or in simple fear of what was going on, wanted to make the impact less, so she wanted to stay away. As you can see from the poem Lynn wrote, which is part of the dedication in this book, Lynn needed to be there at the hospital to see her sister, to know first hand what will forever be with her in memory. She needed to know what has permanently changed her life, her mother's life, her brother Ray's life, and the lives of other relatives.

Jack's 15 year old son, John, had given Lynn a hunting knife which she carried with her, for protection, even in school. She did not know if someone would be after her too. No one then or now knows why Marlys was murdered or who did it. How could she not be afraid? Both Lynn and John laugh about the knife now. But at that time young people were reacting to their fear, fear that was real and justified. Of course, Fran noticed none of this fear at the time.

After the funeral, Fran and her daughter Lynn moved from the hotel to the home of a friend. They could not go back to the house where Marlys was murdered. The murder had not been solved, and so what had been their home was now a place of danger for them. It still remains a place of horror, as the memory of finding Marlys will always be with Fran.

Lynn finished the few days left in her school year, and Fran stayed hidden, with friends, in shock. The first weeks were very painful, and there was no end in sight. The investigation was not leading to an arrest. Suspicions were high. The police talked to everyone even remotely connected to Marlys and the family.

At that time, Fran has said since, she felt totally alone, even among the family and friends who were near. She was so alone that it was as though everyone had been taken from her. Only much later did she notice how alone she was. She felt like Job, whose story is told in the book in the Bible by the same name.

As sad as it is to say, then, when Fran noticed how alone she was, the pain got worse. Others were with her, and still others wanted to be with her and help her, but the pain was hers alone, and she was all alone.

Or was she? If the theology of accompaniment has value, it should show that Fran was not alone, that others were with her. If the theology of accompaniment is really a working theology, thus offering understanding of God's action in our lives, Fran should have noticed. At least, Fran was not as alone as Job.

12

IF GOD PAYS NO ATTENTION

At least Fran was not as alone as one who has lost an entire extended family at one time. She was not alone in the same way that the central character Job is in that book of the Bible. Not only is Job set upon with disease and personal pain, all his children are taken from him.

In the first two chapters of Job, Satan is given permission by God to test Job, almost as in a wager that a faithful servant will endure everything and remain faithful. In Job 1:12, we read,

> *"And the Lord said to Satan, 'Behold, all that he has is in your power; only upon himself do not put forth your hand.' So Satan went forth from the presence of the Lord."*

As part of this test, all of Job's seven sons and three daughters are killed.

This book of the Bible is one of the hardest to read, especially for bereaved parents. Suffering is heaped on a blameless man, and even his children are taken from him. A first reaction from grieving parents is that God has somehow punished Job, and them, by taking away their children. Doesn't the Lord say, "all that he has is in your power" and doesn't Satan take these lives without hesitation?

Is there truth here for the parent whose young son is killed by a drunken driver? Is God testing a parent as leukemia takes a beautiful daughter in her teen years? Was Fran's faith at stake when Marlys was murdered?

These questions and similar ones are not answered by claiming that Job is wrong, or that we can ignore this part of the Bible. We do not even enter into the debate with those who are concerned with what the Bible says about the past. Rather, we seek to find that place where the legitimate promises of Scripture are merged with the experiences of our life. It is in that merger we find understanding, and when we understand, we can give help to others. We ask, "What is said for today, for us?"

What is the expectation that comes from the book of Job in the Bible? Is it that tragedy which comes into our lives, especially when it is unexpected or undeserved in our

79

view, is allowed to happen perhaps because God wants to test us?

We would say that the answer to this question is "NO!" We would say that this is not the expectation that we should take from the Bible. Rather, we believe that Scripture tells us that Job's own expectation was that God would treat him fairly.

Job was blameless, at least as much as any human can be free from blame. The tragedy that befell him was not directly the result of any action or inaction by Job. Job did not understand the source of his misfortune, but he did not have the expectation that God had a reason for allowing it to beset him.

Job was first made into a bereaved parent, as his 10 children were taken from him in a violent death. Then he was inflicted with painful illnesses which drove him to wish he had not been born. His wife and his extended family and his friends were of no comfort. Almost everyone who comments on this book points out how the three friends don't understand. But Job persists in his expectation that God somehow understands, even when his friends and even Job himself does not understand. Eventually, Job meets God and has an opportunity to test this expectation with experience.

Job was perhaps blameless, and we are perhaps not. Job suffers a great loss, of ten children dying a senseless death. We are afflicted by grief when one of our children dies. We know a few parents who have had several children die, and yes, we do not truly understand their grief. But Job is given to us with less blame and more sorrow than most, if not all, have had to bear. Out of his story we can derive expectations.

Primary among these expectations is that we will have our answers from God when we ourselves are standing before God. Before that happens, we will not be given understanding, and others, certainly, will not understand what we feel. The expectation is that we will notice that we are alone, and we will seek answers from God.

*   *   *

One fantasy or dream that many grieving parents have is to imagine that they are able to stand before God and ask, or more often, demand that God tell them why their son or daughter died. The question is not asked intellectually, asking why did the medical treatment fail, or why did my child have to be on that street or in that car at that time. The question that is asked is, "How could you let this happen to my child?"

These are fantasy questions, and we really know the answer, that rain falls on the just and the unjust, and that there is injustice and misery in the world. Our child had bad luck. Even when the child has taken his or her own life, in suicide or reckless or self-destructive conduct, it is really just bad luck. Isn't it?

Our child is dead. Although we may know and even comprehend the medical reasons and the circumstances of what happened at that specific place and time, we can't discount the value of our child's life, saying that it was just bad luck. Luck takes the meaning out of that life, and reduces all life to random happenings. If we continue the fantasy, we ask God why did this life end at this time in this way. What, we ask of God, was your doing in this? If it is just luck, just bad luck for our child and random good luck for the neighboring child, then our lives and our belief in God has no meaning. We would not even bother God for an answer.

* * *

Eventually, Job is allowed to ask his questions of God. Before then, Job is in dialogue with his three friends, and all the answers are tried and fail. Job points to sinners and wicked ones who have a great life, living in glory and wealth to an old age. Moreover, these wicked persons do not suffer the loss of their children. Job sees that the sins of the father do not always visit the sons.

Finally, after 37 chapters, Job has his opportunity to stand before the Lord.

The opportunity to question God for Job evaporates in the whirlwind from which God speaks. God asks the questions, and demands that Job tell him if Job can create universes and defeat monsters and do all wondrous things. Job admits that he cannot.

But is the gloriousness of God and the frailty and failure of humans the only message? Job speaks to God in Job 42:26, saying,

> "I know that thou can'st do all things, and that no purpose of thine can be thwarted. 'Who is this that hides counsel without knowledge?' Therefore I have uttered what I did not understand, things too wonderful for me, which I did not know. 'Hear, and I will speak; I will question you, and you declare to me.' "I had heard of thee by the hearing of the ear, but now my eye sees thee; therefore I despise myself, and repent in dust and ashes."

* * *

Is that all? Perhaps if Fran were more like Job she would be able to stand before God and be humbled, and God would restore her daughter. Chapter 42 ends with Job again having 7 sons and 3 daughters. He died an old man, after seeing his sons, and his sons' sons, four generations.

When Fran faces God, in this life or at the end of her days, it is not unreasonable to expect that a God that can create universes and defeat monsters and do all wondrous things might at that time be understood by Fran, as Job finally understood. When Fran faces God, she too might give up her questions, no longer demanding to know why Marlys was murdered. After all, Marlys will have already had her chance to understand, and perhaps ask the same questions. Marlys has already stood before God.

* * *

The expectation that we get from reading the book of Job is that only when we meet God, not in a whirlwind perhaps, will we have that understanding and only then will we not need to ask questions. We will not need to know why the child we love so much has been taken from us. We will not be concerned with luck. Meeting God will be enough. Job's experience with God merged with his legitimate expectations, and Job found understanding.

Reading Scripture and particularly the book of Job gives us this same legitimate expectation. We too can expect understanding when we experience the presence of God.

The question we have left is this. Do we have to wait until our life as we know it on earth has ended before we have this experience of the presence of God? Is there anything in the book of Job that will give us a real and legitimate expectation that we can experience this presence of God now, here in our grief? Is there anything in Scripture that will give us this answer? Will we have understanding now, before some future time and place about which we may believe but about which we know nothing?

Once again we turn to Scripture, and to the book of Job. In Job's worst misery, as he felt so abandoned, as he noticed that he was in fact alone, Job makes this observation, in Chapter 24, verse 12:

> *"From out of the city the dying groan, and the soul of the wounded cries for help; yet God pays no attention to their prayer."*

In this world, under circumstances of pain and suffering, Job's expectation is that God will answer these prayers of his. Job's experience is that such answer, and an understanding, does not come until one is in the presence of God.

What is our experience? If God pays no attention to the prayers of those whose souls cry for help, to whom do we look for help?

The answer is that those who have been wounded and have somehow survived are called on to respond.

The answer is that we must be there for the newly bereaved, because in being there we meet God. God sent his son, Jesus Christ. Only when we recognize the ministry of accompaniment will we too see God and have understanding in this life, as Job did. We must seek Jesus in those who also need him.

13

UNTIL I STARTED HELPING OTHERS

A 58 year old lawyer friend of ours died in the middle of a struggle with cancer. He was survived by his wife and his brother and his family, and he was also survived by his mother. It is rare when someone lives to be 58 and is survived by a parent, but it happens.

When Jack spoke with the mother, he introduced himself and said that he understood her pain. She just looked at him. Then he said, "We lost our daughter when she was 18." She started to cry, and said, "Then you understand. It hurts so much. I am trying to be brave, for his brother." Jack held her hand, and told her, "I know how it hurts. It will take time. It will take a long time, but others have endured. You will also." She didn't believe him, but thanked him.

Fran will be the first to say that our friend's mother was right. She will never really recover from the loss of a child, even a 58 year old son. But if people acknowledge her pain, and those who have been there show her that they survived, by being there, she will have a chance to heal.

The healing that is necessary if a parent is ever to be able to function after the death of her or his child does take a long time. It is a recovery in a sense, because we do function in society again. It is a recovery also because the scars and the pain are always with us, as when surgery helps us to overcome a disease. We are never the same but, within the limits of the surgery, we are able to function.

The analogy of surgery is very helpful. We need a skilled surgeon and expert doctors to perform the surgery. This is like the comfort and care that other bereaved parents can give. When one who has been in grief and appears to have survived, if not recovered, sits with the newly grieving and offers comfort, recovery can begin.

But we also need the nurses and nurses aides, and we need the other support staff of a hospital, in order to recover. These are the friends and relatives, perhaps not really aware of the pain a parent has in bereavement, but still offering comfort. Someone has to put that cup of tea by your side, just when it is needed.

Over ten years after Marlys was murdered, we were relaxing in our living room with a friend. This friend was a fairly recent acquaintance, and did not know much about us. We had dinner, and were enjoying the new friendship in conversation. During the conversation, as we exchanged stories about our pasts, we started to talk about Marlys's murder. Our friend was interested.

As we talked, we began to tell the story once again, and many memories came back. We were reciting our history, our memory of some event. Jack would say something and Fran would add or correct what he said. Fran would talk about events and Jack filled in what he knew. We felt affirmed that the tragedy of Marlys's murder could again be told, and both could express our feelings.

All through the telling, we made it clear that we had separate roles. Fran's grief was primary but that others, such as Jack, and Fran's other children and Jack's children and all the others had grief and confusion and pain and rejection to deal with as well.

What was interesting about this evening of friendship was that our friend was in the middle of difficult times, and we had invited him over to be of comfort to him. We reached out and had no thought of our own needs. Yet, in our attempt to offer him some comfort, we were comforted. Our new friend showed compassion, and admitted that he didn't know how Fran could have survived Marlys's death. Fran's reply was simple. She said, "I really didn't start healing until I started helping others."

We have made a distinction between recovery and healing. To recover from the death of a child, to the point where we once again can function in society, is one step in the continuing life of those left behind by such a death. It is essential to be able to function, although tragically some people never even reach this state.

To go beyond mere functioning, to once again have meaning in one's life is to experience healing. Helping others is more than functioning, and can become a very positive experience. Helping others can give important meaning to the life that was lost as well as the lives of those who continue. Recovery allows one to function in society. Healing allows others to function better.

The difference between recovery and healing is the difference between being able to say, "I made it through another day," and being able to say, "I feel good about helping another today." Over and over we have said that the grief from the loss of a child is great. We are in great pain, so much that we can't function. We can't go to work, and we can't cook a meal.

In time, particularly with the help of others who have been there, we can go to work, and we can cook a meal. The meal even tastes good. But the pain is still with us. We are still looking inward in our grief.

Eventually, someone who is in pain comes to our attention, and we reach out to help, even by a small gesture. Our pain, even for a moment, is less than what we know the other person is experiencing. We begin to see that our pain is less important than the pain of another, and we let them know that. We start to heal at that time.

* * *

We have said that grief is pain that one cannot physically touch. It is a pain where there is emptiness, as when an arm has been cut off as part of an extreme medical treatment. The arm is gone, and we know it, but we may not consciously think about it every minute of the day. But it is still gone. We can control the rest of our body, and we can learn to live a relatively normal life without that arm.

Yet, we know we will never be the way we were before our loss. We know we are different now, but others forget. Some people expect us to get on with life. They know that it has been several months now, or perhaps several years, and they see us eating just fine with the other hand. They assume everything is good. They may even say to us, "Gee, you don't look like you've lost a child." Inside, we are in pain, missing this child who we used to be able to reach out and touch. We want to hug our child. Be with her. But, how can we hug without our missing arm?

14

WHERE DO I GO TO BE HEALED?

If we are going to use a medical analogy, seeking to understand the absence of a child in our lives, we should ask a question. Where is the hospital? Where is the place where we go to get healing?

Ideally, this place of healing would be the church. That is what a church is for, isn't it? Unfortunately the church does not always function as a place of healing. Unfortunately, there are people in the church who are uncomfortable with those in pain. It is sad to say that many of those parents who have lost a child to death no longer attend church, even if they have recovered and are functioning in other parts of their lives. They stay away, even when they are healing, and helping others in their grief. Why is the church not a place of healing?

This problem, seeking to understand what the church is and what is the proper function of the church, is as old as the church. There are many illustrations we could select in Scripture, and in writings of the many churches in the world, as we try to find these answers. We have selected an event described in Mark 2:15-17, where Jesus is questioned about his table fellowship:

> *And as he sat at table in his house, many tax collectors and sinners were sitting with Jesus and his disciples; for there were many who followed him. And the Scribes and the Pharisees, when they saw that he was eating with sinners and tax collectors, said to his disciples, "Why does he eat with tax collectors and sinners?" And when Jesus heard it, he said to them, "Those who are well have no need of a physician, but those who are sick; I came not to call the righteous, but sinners."*

Simply stated, this text from the Bible demonstrates that the church leaders, the Pharisees, did not understand why Jesus spent time with those outside the established religious community. Many religious leaders see this text as an admonishment to evangelize, to seek out the ones outside the church, to convert nonbelievers. They call on sinners to repent, and develop programs to reach the unsaved.

The religious community is full of good intentions, striving to bring in new members into their churches. Yet, people in grief leave the churches, and we cannot avoid the responsibility to ask why they leave. Why do those who are in pain just seem to attend less often, and still less often, until they no longer attend at all? The same religious leaders who see a call to evangelize do not even think that sinners whom Jesus came to call could be inside the church, needing a physician because they are also sick.

What good does it do to join a church, we ask, if the newly converted find no comfort in the church once they are members? What good does it to be a life-long member of a church, we also ask, if we find no comfort in the church when we are in grief? When we need help, and when they do not even have a basic understanding that there is a need of help, we too will be outside the church.

The sinners which are referred to in the quoted text are outside the church, unclean, not part of the community. If church leaders do not recognize themselves in this text, acting in the same way as the Pharisees, how can we expect them to minister to us in our outside-ness?

We know we hurt, and we know that there are no easy answers. Is it that the religious leaders cannot sit with us, day after day, week after week, year after year, as we express our pain in ways that are often hurtful, if not just plain boring to those who do not feel the pain? Our grief places us outside the church, even when we're in the church building.

Clearly, the typical religious leader has not had the pain and anguish of the loss of a child. Does that mean they cannot understand? Too often the answer is that they cannot or do not understand those who are in grief. And because they don't know what to do, and because they themselves don't know how to find a physician, they give up or ignore the bereaved parents who need help.

Neither the pastor nor priest, nor the elders and deacons and lay leaders know how to deal with those outside the church. After all, if loving Jesus is supposed to bring joy in one's life, why are these people sitting in a back pew, all alone crying? Is it just an embarrassment?

One Protestant pastor we know suffered the loss of his daughter to cancer, and just two weeks later broke down in the pulpit, attempting to preach a normal sermon. Soon after, the church leaders drove him out of that church. They could not understand a pastor who was not comforted, somehow healed because he was a pastor. He was an embarrassment.

Our pastor friend understands how he had become an embarrassment now. He knows there are no easy answers. He knows that a pastor who cannot handle grief is a threat to the church members who have it all figured out, and who have never had that struggle in their own lives. He is still a pastor, actually a much better pastor. When he sees someone outside the church, in the pew or in a coffee shop, he takes the time to be with them. He knows the physician. He knows where the hospital is. Of course! He has been there himself.

There are other exceptions as well. There are churches and pastors and priests who function well at reaching out to the wounded and hurting people of the world. Often these churches have one or more bereaved parents in their leadership community. That is the best resource, to have access to one who has been outside seeking comfort and who has found it.

But there are others who have found ways to reach out. The way that is most effective in reaching and helping those in grief situations is, as we have stressed, to be there, to take all the time that is necessary to sit, to listen, to lend a shoulder. Just as in the text quoted above, the tax collectors and sinners and grieving parents, along with the alcoholics and cocaine addicts and divorced or abused or neglected, are in need of a physician.

Help comes as they sit together, and as the ones who have begun to recover reach out to help those who are less able to cope with their pain. Hurting people really don't start to heal until they start helping others.

*   *   *

People who hurt in the way that bereaved parents hurt have found that their legitimate expectations from life and from God do not coincide with their experience. Yet when we reach out, and begin helping others, we begin to understand that our experiences are correct and are valid. And our experiences can be trusted. When we reach out, and begin to help others, we see that God too has been reaching out. We find as we begin helping others that the presence of God is there with us in the helping.

Hope arises, as now, for the first time the expectations we have from God, from Scripture, from the religious experience, are being experienced in our lives. Let us look for that place of healing, where we might find God.

We have said that our healing did not begin until we started helping others. When we do this, when we lend our shoulder to another who is in greater pain, we begin to surrender our pain in the pain of the other. We are beginning to recognize the ministry of accompaniment. When we accompany those who are in pain, who do not even have what we have, we have begun to find God.

97

Remember the text from Chapter Three, where we quoted from Paul's letter to the Philippians 2:8, which is repeated as follows:

> *And being found in human form, he humbled himself and became obedient unto death, even death on a cross.*

If you expect to find God in the glorious places of this world, you will be disappointed. God is not experienced in all God's glory, with trumpets and angels and all wonderful things, not that way in this world. Just as we found in the last chapter we began to understand the life and struggle that Job endured as Job sought answers from God, we will not find our answers in gold and buildings and splendor.

In this world, if we would seek God, if we would have expectations of comfort, the coincidence of expectation and experience will be found in the life and humanity of Jesus Christ. As Jesus forgot his God-self and became human, and in human form suffered death, we too must forget our self, and reach out to help others. When we are willing to help others, no matter what the cost, we will meet God. Nowhere else.

15

MEMORIALS: A REASON TO DO GOOD

The person who murdered Marlys on that 8th day of May, 1979, is still at large. He, or she, is free and we don't know who that person is. We live with that uncertainty all the time. We don't know why Marlys was murdered. That is another uncertainty with which we are living. Living with all these uncertainties makes for a very crowded house.

Marlys was murdered in the house where she lived, in the beautiful St. Croix Valley, in Afton, Minnesota. She was buried the day before Mother's Day in a cemetery which is part of Memorial Lutheran Church in Afton.

Many people contributed to a reward fund which was to be used to encourage persons who had information about the murder to come forward. No one did. The police in charge of the investigation did as much as they could to find the person who killed Marlys. No one was arrested. We have spent many nights and many days talking about who we suspect. We can't take suspicions into court, however, even when they coincide with the suspicions of the police.

Money from memorial gifts and reward money was used to buy Carillon Chimes for Memorial Lutheran Church. The Carillon bells ring out, every day, loud and clear over the valley of the St. Croix River. The bells sing out loud and clear for everyone to hear.

Our hope is that the person who committed the murder can hear those bells every day. Our hope is that the person is reminded every day that those bells ring in Afton, Minnesota because he or she took the life of another.

Our hope is that the murderer hears those bells, every day, and is reminded of his crime. Our hope is that someday he will realize that he must repent, he must confess that he took a life.

We don't hear those Carillon bells any longer. We moved away from Minnesota, to the east coast. But we often take comfort in knowing that those Carillon bells ring every day, as a memorial to Marlys and others, and as a reminder to her friends who miss her, and as a conscience in the quiet peaceful St. Croix Valley.

The guilt that the murderer feels is hard to measure. We don't know if the person was on drugs, and doesn't remember the crime except for some vague understanding that some bad thing may have been done. We don't know if the person has a constant memory of the act of killing a human being, and is tormented by a conscience. We don't even know whether the murderer is a man or woman, except in our suspicions. There is a lot about this murder that we don't know.

One discussion we have had, together and with friend and family, centers on trying to understand how anyone could have killed Marlys. We don't know how one person could take another person's life under any circumstances. We certainly don't know how one human being can kill another. It doesn't make sense, even after more than 11 years. To even think of standing in the shoes of the murderer is too painful. We can't do it. We will never know what it is like to kill another. In the specific, we ask how anyone can take the life of an 18 year old girl who had no enemies that we know of, no sins hidden from us, no acquaintances who could be that evil. Was it a random event, or an accident or mistake? Was Marlys even the intended victim?

In the abstract, that discussion leads to philosophy and, almost always, to theology. Eventually, we conclude that the person who actually struck the blow committed an irrational act. Normal humans just can't do that kind of violence, unless provoked or in the heat of combat.

We will never be able to understand the one who killed Marlys, even if he confesses. We will never be able to understand that irrational act which makes no sense. It is not possible to put ourselves inside the mind of someone who does all that damage to another human being.

In a way, solving the murder will not make any difference because we still won't understand how someone could do such an act. We ask ourselves how Carillon Chimes will bring such a person to pangs of conscience. We don't even know if it can. We can't understand what affects a conscience when we can't understand what causes such an irrational act as murder.

In the same way, parents of children who die from automobile accidents, plane crashes, suicide, drug overdose, cancer, and all the other causes of death will never understand how such a tragedy could happen. The death of a child happens, by some random event, an accident, a twist of fate. Those things don't have a conscience either.

We are no different than any bereaved parents. Fran' s daughter has been taken from her and no one has answered for that crime. Even if someone confessed tomorrow, and told us why he took Marlys's life, we could not really understand what he said. The death of children from cancer, or car accidents, or suicide, or falling off a mountain, or drowning, or AIDS, or drunk drivers, or starvation, or disease, or poverty, or military exercises, or any other way is a mistake. None of us will understand why, at least not in this life.

More than that, what we have in common with others is that we have no way to understand how God could let that mistake happen any more than parents can have that answer. Even the one who killed Marlys had parents. We know his parents would feel terrible if they knew he killed someone. They might even accept his guilt.

We also know that his parents would not understand why he did it, and they would not understand why he would suffer the death penalty, if that were to happen. We think that they too would ask God why their child had to die. They too would know it is some mistake.

Our conversations together, and our talking with friends and family, and all of the things that form theology have led us to look at events from a different perspective now. Instead of asking how God could let our child die, and instead of asking how God could let any child die, we ask a different question. Where is God in this?

We don't hold God responsible for Marlys's murder. God didn't use the blunt instrument and strike her down. God doesn't directly cause the death of any child. We don't ask why God caused the death of children from cancer, or car accidents, or suicide, or falling off a mountain, or drowning, or AIDS, or drunk drivers, or starvation, or disease, or poverty, or military exercises, or any other way. Rather than ask why, we ask the question, "Where is God in this?"

We know that individual human beings cause the death of others. We know that natural events, like earthquakes and hurricanes cause death. We know that disease and poverty and oppression cause death. Social conditions can cause the death of children, in Ethiopia and El Salvador and the ghettos of Philadelphia. We do not know that God causes death.

Perhaps the Carillon bells ring for our conscience, as a reminder that there is much that we can do to help others who are in greater need that we are. There are so many causes of death, and so few sources of life. The memorials, the Carillon bells are a reason to do good.

16

THE MEMORIAL GAVE US HOPE

When one reads the Bible, it is easy to find examples of death and destruction, sometimes with justice and sometimes of those who we would consider innocent. When an entire group of people are killed, as one can read in the Bible, particularly the Old Testament, it appears that God has caused these deaths.

A review of each such instance in the Bible is beyond the scope of this book. However, it is important that each bereaved parent and everyone else, for that matter, resolve this question. When one goes to the Bible for comfort or for understanding or for whatever reason, one should look at the stories and teachings seriously. It is helpful, we are suggesting, particularly for bereaved parents but also for everyone else to ask the right questions. Let us look at just one example.

The Book of Judges in the Bible describes one of the really bad people in all of human recollection. Sisera was a really bad man and he killed many innocent people. Chapter Four of Judges starts by telling us that the Lord sold the people of Israel into the hand of Jabin, the king of Canaan, because they had done evil in the sight of the Lord. Sisera was the commander of the army and he "oppressed the people of Israel cruelly for twenty years."

Deborah, a prophetess and judge of Israel, tells Barak, who has an army of liberation, that *"the Lord will sell Sisera into the hand of a woman."* This certainly seems to say that God has had a hand in these events.

Still in Chapter Four of Judges, Sisera comes to the tent of Jael, the wife of Heber, one who was at peace with Sisera's king. Jael offers him rest in her tent, and Sisera accepts. As the chapter ends, Sisera tells Jael to *"Stand at the door of the tent, and if any man comes and asks you, 'Is any one here?' say, No."* Then we learn that Jael took a tent peg, and took a hammer in her hand, and drove the peg into his temple, till it went down into the ground. So Sisera died.

Jael then finds Barak, who is pursuing Sisera, and takes him to her tent to find Sisera dead, with the tent peg in his temple. The chapter ends by saying that, *"So on that day God subdued Jabin the king of Caanan before the people of Israel."*

Chapter Five is the "Song of Deborah" which is a poetic reflection on her role as a judge and prophetess. Beginning at verse 24, Deborah's poetic song tells the story of Sisera's death at the hand of Jael. At this point, it seems that God has had a major role in the events leading to relief from oppression. But we do not overlook verse 28, as we read Judges 5:24-28:

> *Most blessed of women be Jael, the wife of Heber the Kenite, of tent-dwelling women most blessed. He asked water and she gave him milk, she brought him curds in a lordly bowl. She put her hand to the tent peg and her right hand to the workmen's mallet; She struck Sisera a blow, she crushed his head, she shattered and pierced his temple. He sank, he fell, he lay still at her feet; at her feet he sank, he fell; where he sank, there he fell dead.*

and verse 28

> *Out of the window she peered, the mother of Sisera gazed through the lattice: "Why is his chariot so long in coming? Why tarry the hoofbeats of his chariots?"*

There are many forms of biblical interpretation. All that we ask here is that we recognize that Sisera's mother's anguish is recorded in the Song of Deborah. Is it a memorial to an evil man? We don't think so. But it might be a memorial to the grief that every parent has when his or her own child dies and that mother or father is left to grieve.

We don't suggest that Sisera should not have died, especially in that time in history when violent death was expected. We don't suggest that Jael is any less a blessed woman to Israel's history, for she clearly helped save many lives with her act. Deborah did the right thing, we think, in praising Jael. We also suggest that Deborah did the right thing when she recorded a memorial to the grief of Sisera's mother.

We think that the Bible speaks to recognition of grief, and to the presence of God in that grief. Biblical events and the present days both show us that God is active in human lives. Our need now is to understand that God is with us, and with everyone, in their grief.

* * *

To us, the Carillon bells do not toll forgiveness over the St. Croix River valley in Afton, Minnesota. The message that is sent, we hope, is that God, through the church and also without the consenting knowledge of the church, is with us in our grief. We also hope that the one who killed Marlys hears those bells, and is brought to repent. We also hope that his mother and father, if either are alive and in the valley, also know that God will be with them when their time comes.

Memorials are a fine thing and should be erected, with dignity, for the memory of the child who has gone on before us. But memorials are not the answer. Memorials, even as great as the pyramids in Egypt, are no substitute for the child who has died. Marlys is worth more to Fran than all the bells in the world, now and ever.

But, at least, we are looking out at the world rather than totally in at our grief. We are hoping that someone will notice our grief. We are like Sisera's mother, standing at the window, looking for our child, hoping for the hopeless.

* * *

Memorials serve to give us hope by helping us to look out at the world, but we need something beyond memorials if we are to go beyond our grief. We receive hope from memorials, and we need that hope to move on. We will never forget our child, but we do no good to that child's memory if our grief destroys us and if we are not somehow able to help others.

We turn again to the Bible for understanding. This time we are not looking for a story, but for perhaps a definition. What is the hope that we would get? Listen to these words from the Bible. Romans 8:24-25 says:

> *For in this hope we were saved. Now hope that is seen is not hope. For who hopes for what he sees? But if we hope for what we do not see, we wait for it with patience.*

Certainly this definition is true for bereaved parents. Our hope is that our child is with God. That is what prevents us from total despair. Our child has now seen the majesty of God, like Job, and all is well for Marlys.

Whatever we hope for cannot be seen. If we hope that memorials will heal our grief, we are hoping for something that we cannot see. If the memorials help us to turn outward, from ourselves and our grief, toward others, then our hope really is that God is with us. And while we cannot see God, not directly and face to face, we hope.

We hope that God is with the one who set in motion that mistake that killed Marlys. We hope that God is speaking, louder than the Carillon bells, calling him to repentance. We are able to get anger out, and to take vengeance however briefly by having bells ring in the ears of Marlys's killer. We are

110

hoping, guessing really, that we have done something.

The memorial gave us hope that justice would be done, that the truth would come out, and that we could do something to punish the one who killed her. This isn't a pure motive. It isn't what Christ would do. But, just as God lets us know that Sisera's mother waits and mourns, God is with the one who hears the Carillon bells in that tiny Minnesota town. Maybe he will repent.

* * *

There are other forms of memorials which do good and which are also used by bereaved parents as a necessary and legitimate outlook for the anger and hurt and despair they suffer. Memorials tell the story that we have been deprived of our child and we hurt. We want others to know that, and because we want to recover in some way from the intense pain we feel, we want to do some good.

Money is given as a memorial, for cancer research or hospitals and hospice programs, and for rescue equipment. Bereaved parents work to stop others from drunken driving, or to change safety laws on college campuses, or to have dangerous products removed from the market. Beautiful stained glass windows provide beauty in a church. Smaller, equally precious gifts are given, sometimes anonymously to the recipient, but always with the thought that somehow we are keeping alive the memory of one whom we miss greatly, so that others will remember our child too.

If we didn't have memorials, we wouldn't have anything to say. We would have no hope, even in things we can see or hear or touch. But we do have hope. We have reached out, to tell the world of our pain, and we have started to heal. We will never recover, but we are healing with the scar and with the memory of our child. We hope. We start to heal.

Now we ask, what does this mean and where does it lead?

17

TEN YEARS TO UNDERSTAND, ALMOST

As this book was being written, we celebrated the eleventh Christmas after Marlys died. We are on the east coast now, far from Minnesota, and we had a bad day about a week before Christmas.

Fran had been planning on taking decorations to Marlys's grave, and needed some help clearing snow. Jack wanted to help buy the decorations, and had suggested stopping several times when it was not possible. Fran had bought them when Jack was at his office. After dinner that day, the bad day got worse. Both of us had hurt feelings and old pains came back for a little while.

Both of us came to our senses, fortunately, because this had happened before, and we were able to go to the grave and place the wreath in just the right place. It looked nice, and at Christmas we came back and lit the candle we took from the candlelight church service we attended on Christmas Eve. We got through the bad day because we understand that there are sensitive feelings, especially at holidays and anniversaries. After all, we had been having good and bad days for the last eleven years, and we understand, almost.

We have said that we will never recover from Marlys's murder, but we are healing, with scars and with the memories we have. We are healing because we have hope which has come from reaching out to tell the world of our pain. From that hope, we need to see progress, so that we can be reminded that we are healing.

We recently looked at the picture that was taken of us on the first Christmas, as we posed by the tree. The best thing that can be said about the picture is that we can see just how far we have come. There is comfort in physical proof that healing takes place, outwardly, so that others can see it. This is the experience bereaved parents have when they reach out to newly-bereaved. There is comfort in helping the newly bereaved, just by being there and saying that they understand. As a mother reaches out to others, she sees herself as she was at first. Nobody wants to look that bad.

If we could describe ourselves then in that Christmas photo, we would say that Fran looked like she was in great pain, which she was, of course. Photos of Fran now don't show that pain, as it is covered over with the scars of healing. The best pictures of Fran now are taken when she is helping others or is talking about her efforts to help those in pain.

*   *   *

Fran was not married to Marlys's father when Marlys was murdered, and she has not had to deal directly with this very real concern that bereaved parents have to deal with. Fran's marriage to Marlys's father, Jim Wohlenhaus, ended 14 years before Marlys's death in 1979. Both Fran and Jim had other relationships that were more important in 1979, and each has continued on those separate paths taken years earlier.

This does not mean that their divorce prevented them from additional pain, as one parent sees another suffering in the loss of the child. But after the funeral, each of them went back to those separate paths to seek comfort and healing in different ways. They had neither the advantages nor the disadvantages that belong to a couple who are together when a child of their marriage dies.

Perhaps the majority of the time, however, both parents suffer the pain and grief of the death of a child together, in the marriage that brought that child into this world. How can one spouse help one's partner recover when he or she is in so much need of help? The answer is that some do survive together and some do not.

We have seen statements that many of the parents of children who have died get a divorce, but that has not been our experience. Our experience is that the divorce rate for bereaved couples whom we know and meet is lower than the divorce rate of other couples. Of course, our experience is with bereaved couples who are helped by others and are helping others.

These are couples who reach out, who find hope in memorials and in working for others. In their pain and grief, they have one advantage, and that is they understand what the other is experiencing. If they hang on, not taking their anger out on each other, and if there is love for the other, they can survive together and have an even stronger marriage. The healing process is the same. Reaching out to another in pain and grief is absolutely essential for healing of self. If you can reach out to your spouse, and many do, this is a great act of love.

The traditional understanding of love between couples as expressed in the Bible comes from Paul's First Letter to the Corinthians, in Chapter 13. This is often read at marriage services, and is known as the "love chapter." It is, we think, even more appropriate to read these words now in an attempt to understand what is needed for the marriage to survive the death of a child. It would be worthwhile reading the entire 13th Chapter of First Corinthians. The last two verses are particularly relevant. First Corinthians 13:12-13 says:

> *For now we see in a mirror dimly, but then face to face. Now I know in part; then I shall understand fully, even as I have been fully understood. So faith, hope, love abide, these three; but the greatest of these is love.*

* * *

There is a great opportunity for couples who seek to survive together in this most horrible grief when their child dies, to reach out in love to the partner with whom they joined together in love to bring this child into this world. For most couples, this leads to healing for both partners.

Those couples who are not successful in staying together after a child dies often say that the marriage was bad anyway. We believe them, for without a strong bond of love there will not be enough reaching out for the other.

Each will dwell on his or her own pain and grief, and when they don't reach out to the other, when even one does not reach out to the other, the self comes first. There is no healing in that.

Perhaps they will find another partner who will love them and will want to be loved by them. Perhaps that will have happened before the child dies, and perhaps that will happen after. In that new relationship, comfort and healing will come, if it does, when both partners in that new relationship reach out to love and comfort the other, rather than dwell on their own feelings.

Understanding will come in time if there is enough love. They will be glad if they can even see in a mirror dimly. The love chapter of First Corinthians will have special meaning for them as they seek to understand the grief and the hope that love can give for healing, scars and all.

18

WHAT DO STEP-PARENTS KNOW?

In the photograph from our first Christmas after Marlys's death, Jack looked both concerned and confused. He has tried for eleven years to understand, and he says that most of the confusion is gone. But the concern remains. Jack says that he forgets, and then, all of a sudden, he remembers to be concerned because Fran is having a bad moment, perhaps experiencing a memory.

Being there, and listening when it is hard to hear the same things over and over is very difficult, but it is absolutely essential in the first few years. That job isn't ever over, and it's always important to have that sensitive ear ready to listen to the pain come out. Eventually, it is even possible to draw out the pain, knowing when to ask about a bad day.

The step-parent has to remember that he or she has not experienced the mind-numbing grief, when the mind slams shut and nothing penetrates the consciousness except the pain of the loss of the child. The step-parent has to understand that his or her love is not a substitute for the child, and never will be a substitute.

The step-parent has to understand something that is impossible to understand, and at the same time must repress his or her own feelings. It is especially hard to repress feelings of impatience and of being excluded. These are two of the hardest emotions to ignore.

It is easy to say, or even think that it is time that my spouse was over this grief thing. Think it, then forgive yourself for not understanding, and then do something nice for your spouse. Never say it. It isn't true, in the first place, and it isn't up to you to decide anyway.

It is also easy to claim some right to be included in the grief process. Step-parents have feelings too, and it is natural to want to assert them. Do that when the events relate to your life together, gently, but don't ask to be part of the problem. Your spouse needs someone who will provide the love until that time when he or she can give love in return. Be part of the solution, loving, putting the other ahead of one's self.

A step-parent will have grief as well, as one who knew the love of the child partly perhaps, and who now can never have that love. Several times, Jack has said that he wishes that Marlys was here to brighten his day. He will never again have that experience with Marlys, any more than Fran will. His loss leads to a small understanding of what Fran feels every day.

Even if the child died before the step-parent came to know and love his grieving spouse, some vital part of that mother or father is missing, forever. The step-parent has a loss of experiences which might have led to pleasant memories. Dealing with that lack will lead to an understanding of the loss kept in the memories of the child's parent.

On bad days, the step-parent will feel left out, perhaps mistakenly, and will want to be part of something that he or she doesn't qualify to be part of. On our bad day, just before our eleventh Christmas after Marlys died, we learned once again to share our feelings. After eleven years, it is legitimate to talk about participation in memories. After eleven years, it is a good day when we go to the cemetery together and light a candle. We both said that night that we have gone beyond cursing the darkness.

* * *

If step-parents really understood, they would always be there at the right time, ready to listen and be there. We say this because the only way to fully love is to give oneself fully for another. Only when we give ourselves to another do we express our love in a way that is meaningful. Only when we forget our own needs and tend to the needs of others are we truly expressing love and not self gratification. This is the message of Jesus which we have found, to love as it is said in the Gospel of John 3:16-17. As you read these verses, try to keep in mind that God is a bereaved parent.

> *For God so loved the world that he gave his only Son, that whoever believes in him should not perish but have eternal life. For God sent the Son into the world, not to condemn the world, but that the world might be saved through him.*

It is hard to translate this Bible text to the reality that is experienced by bereaved parents. Certainly no one would send a child to die for others. Even in war time, the expectation is that our child will come home safely. Even in times of heroism, we wish that someone else would have given his or her life instead of our child dying for others, no matter how many others are saved. We can't think of loving anyone enough so that we would give up our son or daughter for any reason. Then what does the text tell us?

We would give up our own life if we could save the life of our son or daughter. Fran has said that she truly wishes that she had died in Marlys's place, if only Marlys would be alive. Fran would trade her life for Marlys brought back to life today.

This is a common desire in bereaved parents. This is an expression of love for another, if not for all others, at least on a human scale. But on the human level we have no hope that our child will return, even in our place. Despite our love for our child, there is nothing in which we can place our faith that such a miracle would happen.

But if we have faith in God, we can have hope because such a miracle did happen. The miracle is the total self denial of God in Jesus Christ, who suffered death on a cross. Christ who was God took on human form so that we all can have eternal life, and this was done out of love. God expressed that love on a divine level when God sent the Son into the world, that the world would be saved and not condemned. God's gift of his Son is a gift of self that teaches us the meaning of life itself.

We have our faith, out of which comes hope, so that we might love, for in love we will find the answer. We would die that our child would live. Jesus Christ died that we all shall live. We need to understand, in a mirror dimly, perhaps, that humanity has been fully understood by God in the life, death and resurrection of Jesus Christ. What we know in part we will understand fully when we too stand before God.

19

CHRIST IS THE CHALLENGE

Our goal as we seek to heal the grief and pain of Marlys's death is not that we somehow fully recover from her death. We don't expect that we will be happy and untroubled. We can't deny the value of her life and her very personhood. Marlys's death means a great deal to us, and it always will, because her life meant so much. Now, in this life at least, all we have is our memory of her. That must be preserved.

In the first year after Marlys died, we both went to the cemetery at the little white church on the hill. Fran took pleasure in tending her grave, placing flowers and decorations, making it look nice. Jack stood and watched, and lifted the heavy things. We knew that her body was still in the casket, but we did not consider that Marlys had a presence at the cemetery.

In 1985, six years after Marlys was murdered and almost five years after we moved to Pennsylvania, we moved Marlys's grave. We moved the casket, and had a small grave-side service with family and friends, because Fran wanted to continue tending the grave and making it nice. It felt right to do and we did it. It still feels right.

Our lives reflect our loss of Marlys, and our expression of that loss includes making visits to a cemetery, to a monument of stone, and to a buried casket so that Fran can tend things and make it nice. It isn't enough, but it is something. There is a peace that comes from having a place to go, in this world, and we think, in the life to come.

Marlys's personality, her spirit, her soul is with God, and will remain there until the end times. What those end times mean and what will happen then we do not understand. It is no more within our knowledge now than it was for Jesus, or for his closest disciples.

Even when Jesus was on the cross, when the criminals who were hanging with him said,

> *"Jesus, remember me when you come into your kingdom,"*

Jesus replied, in the Gospel of Luke, Chapter 23, verse 43:

> *"And he said to him, 'Truly, I say to you, today you will be with me in Paradise.'"*

Every bereaved parent believes that his or her child is with Jesus now. We have no doubt that this is true. We will not be fully healed, however, until we are with Marlys and Jesus, or rather Jesus and Marlys. That day is not this day.

*   *   *

What we know for sure is that if life as we know it is going to have any meaning, if reality is going to exist for us, that will happen as we keep the memory of our child alive. To make life a reality, Christ challenges us through helping others, so that the memory of our child never dies. Christ is the challenge.

We can not just sit back and let ourselves die. No bereaved parent should do that. We want our child to live eternally. We have a desire to do something, to preserve our child's life in memory. The only way a child will live is through the work that we do, helping others. If we turn in on ourselves, we are not responding to that challenge of Christ.

What will we say, then, when we stand before God? The only time we will ever have Marlys back with us, to laugh and tease and play and work and love, will be when we stand before God in the end times. Marlys will be standing there with us, and we will have answers to those questions that we ask in vain now.

Our promise, that we take from the Bible, from God who entered into history, is that there will be judgment. We will stand before God, as Job did, and we will understand all. But that is then, and this is now. Now, we have the life and the death and the resurrection of Jesus Christ. We are challenged to follow that life if we are to participate in it fully.

* * *

We have said before that Jesus Christ forgot his God-self and became human, and in human form suffered death on a cross. We also said that this means, at least in part, that we must be willing to die in order to have comfort in our pain. We must be willing to die for others, not for ourselves, for there is no obedience and humility in that.

In the Letter to the Philippians, we have already read of the actions of Christ. Listen to what Paul also has written, this time about his own understanding of the challenge of Christ. In Philippians 3:8-11, Paul writes:

Indeed I count everything as loss because of the surpassing worth of knowing Christ Jesus my Lord. For his sake I have suffered the loss of all things, and count them as refuse, in

*order that I may gain Christ and be
found in him, not having a
righteousness of my own, based on law,
but that which is through faith in
Christ, the righteousness from God that
depends on faith; that I may know him
and the power of his resurrection, and
may share his suffering, becoming like
him in his death, that if possible I may
attain the resurrection from the dead.*

All of us would be like Paul in wanting
the resurrection from the dead. Not all of us
are like Paul in wanting to become like Christ
in his death, however, and this is the
challenge that we face. If we are to be like
Christ, and like what Paul wants to be, we
must accept the whole challenge. In order to
share in the resurrection, Paul understands
that he must share in Christ's suffering,
becoming like him in his death.

* * *

If we do not have faith in the
resurrection, then all we have is this world at
this time, with only the memory of our child.
It is so sad when all one has is a memory. But
if we do have faith in the resurrection, and in
the challenge to live for others rather than
ourselves, we have the hope that we too will
become like Christ and Paul and our child,
and attain the resurrection from the dead.

Some people who read the Bible say that Jesus was abandoned by God while he was on the cross. Certainly the plaintive cry recorded in Mark 15:34 and Matthew 27:46, leads one to think that the human Jesus at least felt alone:

"My God, My God, why hast thou forsaken me?"

But Luke's Gospel reports in Luke 23:46, that Jesus said:

"Father, into thy hands I commit my spirit!"

John's Gospel simply reports in John 19:30 that Jesus said:

"'It is finished'; and he bowed his head and gave up his spirit."

We as Christians believe that Jesus was not only human but was and is also God, together with the Holy Spirit, in some way that we do not fully understand but have named the Trinity. And we as bereaved parents believe that God was not absent when Jesus died. God was silent, but present, just as we are to be present for others who suffer in this world.

Our theology, if it has a name, is a Theology of Accompaniment. Being there for others, even being silent when there is nothing to say, is part of our theology. But there is more to accompaniment than just being there. Accompaniment means being willing to place others ahead of one's self when they are more in need of comfort.

Taken to its logical conclusion, accompaniment includes a willingness to die for others, that others may live. This is what Christ did and this is what most parents would do for their children. We would die that our child could live, because we love our child. God took on human form and died on the cross that humanity might have eternal life, because God so loved the world.

This is how comfort from God coincides with the experience of living for God. This is the challenge of Christ.

20

ACCEPTING THE CHALLENGE

Accepting the challenge of Christ is not simply a matter of saying something and being done with it. It is necessary to love someone, another actually, enough to lay down one's life. And we can't do that for our child. We need to find a way to merge our expectation of being healed, in Christ, with an experience that makes the healing real for us. How does this happen?

One person whose story demonstrates a merger of expectation and experience is a doctor we met in the mountains of a Latin American country. This doctor, a native of Latin America who was educated in Europe, had been an atheist at one time in her life. Not long before we first met her, a nurse had been killed while giving vaccinations to children. Since no one else would go to continue the work, this doctor began to administer the vaccinations herself, without a nurse.

Walking with a thermos of vaccine over one shoulder and a rifle over the other shoulder, she seeks to bring health to those who have a great need for her help. She says that she is no longer an atheist and that she has come to know what Jesus meant when he said, "They do not take my life from me, it is mine to give."

This doctor has taken the words of John 10:17-18, and given them new meaning. Let us read those words of Jesus:

"For this reason the Father loves me, because I lay down my life, that I may take it again. No one takes it from me, but I lay it down of my own accord. I have power to lay it down, and I have power to take it again; this charge I have received from my Father."

Her life could end soon, if it hasn't already, and yet she is turned toward God, facing God, with such clarity that she sees no contradiction between God's word and her own life. This is accompaniment.

* * *

There is another story which is more personal. Fran visited another Latin American country, El Salvador, in 1978, the year before Marlys was murdered. Fran was a tourist who saw a beautiful countryside and

132

beautiful people. She says quite honestly that she fell in love with El Salvador.

In March of 1987, Fran again traveled to El Salvador, this time to walk with the Mothers of the Disappeared as they commemorated the death of Archbishop Oscar Romero. She went as part of an ecumenical group to celebrate Romero's death as a victory over the forces of evil. She went to participate in the delivery of a nation that she loves, El Salvador, a delivery by the hands of God.

Fran also went to deal with her own grief, in solidarity with those who would understand. She walked and prayed and worshipped with several hundred Mothers of the Disappeared. These mothers know the pain of loss when their children are taken from them, killed, and are left to be found on body dumps. When they were in the Basilica in San Salvador, praying to God for an end to the war, helicopters hovered above the church. Their rotors beat down on the church, beating with intimidation. When Fran came home, she admitted that during the worship service, at least, she would have put herself between the mothers and anyone intruding with a gun, to prevent arrests from being made.

Fran's testimony is very much like that of the Apostle Paul, who we paraphrase from his second letter to the Corinthians, that in the hardships she underwent in (Asia or Minnesota or El Salvador) we should be quite certain that she was under extraordinary pressure. It was beyond her powers of endurance, so that she gave up hope of surviving. But she did survive in her accompaniment. God was a comfort, not from a hidden place on high, but from the understanding of those who had been comforted by the presence of those who understood.

*   *   *

Those moments of accompaniment do not last forever. Emotional lifting up in solidarity with others who have survived, somehow, a very bad event is part of the process of forming scars. As we heal from our own tragedy and bereavement, we can help others. We can tell our own story . We can listen to the story of others. Most importantly, we can reach out to others in love.

The only way to oppose suffering is to be there and to accompany the ones who are suffering. We should read God's word, and we should pray, of course. But we should take the time to sit in silence and acknowledge the grief and the loss. We should be there for those who do not understand why God has allowed this personal tragedy to occur, and help them to find others who have survived.

As one is comforted, particularly by the presence of someone who has already been there, hope will arise out of the faith that God too is present. Hope becomes complete as the one who is suffering learns to help others more newly bereaved. There is a surrender of one's own pain in the pain of another.

As Jesus Christ says in John 13:34:

> *A new commandment I give to you, that you love one another, even as I have loved you, that you also love one another.*

If we accept the challenge of Christ, to love others as he has loved us, we will be healed. In this life we will give honor to the memory of our child, given in love. When finally we stand before God, we and our child will be fully healed in God's love.

Reach out in peace.

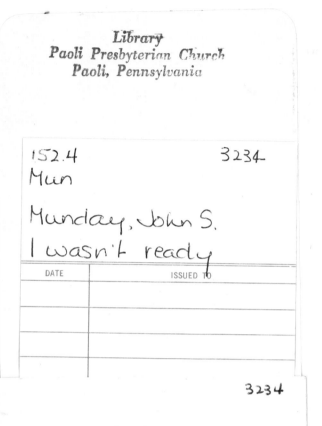